BIBLE THERAPY

How the Bible Solves Your Problems:
A Guide to God's Word

E. C. Wittman
and C. R. Bollman

toExcel
San Jose New York Lincoln Shanghai

Bible Therapy
How the Bible Solves Your Problems: A Guide to God's Word

Published by toExcel
an imprint of iUniverse.com, Inc.

For information address:
iUniverse.com, Inc.
620 North 48th Street
Suite 201
Lincoln, NE 68504-3467
www.iuniverse.com

ISBN: 0-595-09557-7

Printed in the United States of America

Contents

Introduction

What is *Bible Therapy*, and how can it help you?

Today, seemingly as never before, many people are conducting a search for deep, inner emotional peace. You may be one of these people.

But do you have years, or perhaps a lifetime, to give to this search? Of course not. You need to find peace and help and tranquillity right now.

Possibly, because of your eagerness for answers, you may have gone far afield in your search. It is no secret that many people have looked to such ideas and organizations as TM® and EST, while others have investigated East Indian philosophy or other forms of Eastern religion or culture.

But why look to such distant sources of spiritual help when the Bible, the truest and the best source of comfort, is so close at hand?

Of course, if you are not a student of the Bible or theology, you may have found it difficult to use the Holy Scriptures to gain the help and the guidance you need quickly.

That is the reason for *Bible Therapy*.

Within the pages that follow, you will find the help you are searching for. Simply turn to the pages that list your particular problem, be it fear, alcoholism, loneliness, temptation, or any of a number of others; on those pages you will find passages and parables from the Bible that apply directly to your personal problem—passages and parables that are meant to apply directly to your individual need.

The words of the Bible have not been changed within Bible Therapy. In some cases, the spelling has been modernized for easier reading, but these are the actual words, the holy words, the words that have been passed down to us through the centuries. But the passages are so delineated, separated, and arranged that you can find the aid and the comfort you need when you need it.

Now you can use the Bible as it has always been meant to be used. It is your book, and it was intended to give you help and guidance. But instead of having to spend many hours, or weeks, or perhaps even months, searching through the Holy Scriptures for passages that are appropriate and meaningful to you, you can find the help you need quickly within the pages of *Bible Therapy.*

Bible Therapy covers many subjects, many problems that harass us today. Each problem is followed by pages of applicable passages from the Bible—passages that will, hopefully, give you immediate peace and solace.

Use *Bible Therapy* the way you would a good friend, a friend whom you can consult when you are worried or troubled or frightened. It will not have all the answers, true, but it will open a door for you, and it can help you toward finding faith and happiness and the ultimate answers to all of life's problems.

Most of all, it is hoped that *Bible Therapy* will help you to realize that you are never really alone. At the darkest moment, the most depressing hour, help is at hand. Reach out your hand to grasp it—it has always been waiting for you.

What Bible Therapy
Can Do for You

BY DR. J. C. MACAULEY

The coauthors of this book have not written as theologians, nor yet as philosophers. Rather, they have written as women who have experienced "the comfort of the Scriptures" in the rough and tumble of this world, and who wish to share their comfort with others in "life's mad race." The comments are brief, intended to introduce the Scripture passages, which are allowed to speak for themselves.

The primary use of this volume will be very personal. Many will find their own needs reflected here, with appropriate Scriptures for guidance, strength, hope, and solace. But there will be other uses. Young pastors will learn to apply the Word to the varied needs of their flock. It could also add an important dimension to the therapeutic ministry of the Christian psychiatrist.

Bible-taught people will doubtless think of other passages which could answer the various situations listed here, for the Bible is inexhaustible. Actually, the chief value of this book will not be in the authors having chosen the suitable texts for us, but in showing us how to dig the golden nuggets from the rich mine of Holy Scripture.

New York, 1977

EDITOR'S NOTE

Dr. J. C. Macauley was a Pastor at the Wheaton Bible Church, Wheaton, Illinois. During his pastorate, Wheaton College con-

9

ferred on him the honorary degree of Doctor of Divinity. He has taught at the Moody Bible Institute in the fields of evangelism and theology. Dr. Macauley is the foimer President of the London College of Bible and Missions, London, Ontario, Canada. During the past thiee and a half years, Dr. Macauley served as Interim Minister of the Calvary Baptist Church in New York City and his Sunday services were a favorite of many radio listeners.

At present, Dr. Macauley is Dean of the New York School of the Bible.

Dr. Macauley is author of a number of books, including *Personal Evangelism.*

The Bible's Place
in Today's World

The Bible is the one book that is never out-of-date. Frequently, books are published that are purported to be "the very last word" on a variety of subjects. But when it comes to the most important subjects of all—love, peace, and salvation—the Bible is both the *first* and the *last* word, the most important document of all time.

True, the Bible was written many centuries ago, but yet, the Bible is never out-of-date. How can it be out-of-date when it is the Word of God? And that Word is as meaningful and applicable today as it was during the days when it was recorded for the very first time.

Perhaps you are thinking that centuries ago there were no motorcars, no airplanes, no radios or television, no atomic bombs. Now there are these, and many other factors, creating pressure from without and impinging on our lives.

But it is not these outward manifestations of life in the twentieth century that cause our problems. It is, rather, the pressures from within—the pressures from our heads and our hearts that make us sad, or worried, or anxious—it is the need to cope with these pressures that make us look to that living treasure, the Holy Bible.

Is the Bible old-fashioned? Does it contain scientific error? No, it does not, which is yet another indication that the inspiration to write the Bible was Heaven-sent.

Ancient peoples, such as the Egyptians and the Babylonians, did have their own scientific interpretation of the world around them, but the Bible does not report these errors in scientific thought. The Bible is free from such errors, because as the Word of God it was inspired and, therefore, no errors were recorded.

Throughout the centuries, people have respected the Bible. Believers have understood that the Bible was a personal message, to each of them inspired by God. There is the famous story about Sir Walter Scott, who, when he lay dying, asked his son-in-law to bring him the Book.

The son-in-law was puzzled. There were so many books in Sir Walter's home that he didn't know which volume the poet and writer was referring to.

"There is just one Book," Sir Walter replied to his son-in-law's question, and with that his son-in-law brought him the Bible.

This incident has been immortalized in the verses of an anonymous poet:

> "There's just one Book," cried the dying sage,
> "Read me the old, old story."
> And the winged words that can never age
> Wafted him home to Glory.
> There's just one Book.
>
> There's just one Book for life's gladness,
> One Book for the toilsome days,
> One Book that can cure life's madness,
> One Book that can voice life's praise.
> There's just one Book.

There is just one Book—one Book that contains all the wisdom and spiritual values that we need today, in the twentieth century.

Actually, the Bible is like a vast ocean, containing so much within its depths that one could read and consult it constantly, without completely ferreting out every last, brilliant nugget.

The Bible is the helping hand of God, forever being offered. That is why when people are puzzled, perplexed, or troubled, they turn to the one Book, and that is the reason behind *Bible Therapy.*

The word *therapy* comes from the Greek *therapeia,* which means healing. Today, therapy is often interpreted as having only one meaning, and that is healing offered through psychology and psychiatry. But that is far too narrow a definition for a word as vast as therapy.

Healing methods can take on many forms, depending on the illness that requires the cure, and the Bible can certainly be employed therapeutically when it comes to healing the ills of the soul and the spirit.

Do you experience extreme fear from time to time? You may be fearful about the future, about your family, about your faith, about dying. Everyone suffers from fears and anxieties at various times in his life.

But you need not face these fears alone! The Bible contains answers for every one of your fears. Written by forty authors over a period of fifteen hundred years, the Bible speaks to you today, just as it spoke at the time it was written. It is the Word, and as Jesus said,

If a man loves me, he will keep my words.

JOHN 14:23

Perhaps you want to keep His words; you know that the Bible is revelation from God, but the Bible, though a treasure trove, may be bewildering to you.

There is so much in the Bible that its very richness confuses. When you have a problem and want solace, you go to the Bible, but once you hold the Book in your hands, you may need a guide, someone or something to indicate the way.

Think of *Bible Therapy* as that guide, a helping hand which will point out the various paths to you in a friendly, but vast, country. That is what *Bible Therapy* is intended to do.

The words of the Bible have not been changed; they are offered to you just as they come to all of us through the centuries. As it is said,

> Heaven and earth shall pass away, but my words shall not pass away.
>
> MATTHEW 24:35

Bible Therapy is another way of gaining help from the Bible. The Bible offers infinite help and solace for every problem imaginable. *Bible Therapy* has taken as many problems as possible in one volume, and under various headings has offered suggested passages that may help you in time of trouble.

The Bible is infinite, but *Bible Therapy* is not. No book, other than the Book, can be. But *Bible Therapy* opens a door, shines a light, tries to show the many ways the Bible can help you find peace and comfort.

Bible Therapy may lead you on to find new answers. You may discover that once you have used this book as a guide, you can go on by yourself, the treasures of the Bible becoming more available to you.

Look to the Bible when you are troubled, in doubt, or are suffering from fear or anxiety. The Bible has all the answers, and *Bible Therapy* can help you find them.

The Word is a great gift, given by a loving Father to His children,

> The grass withereth, the flower fadeth: but the word of our God shall stand for ever.
>
> ISAIAH 40:8

BIBLE THERAPY

O give thanks unto the Lord; call upon his name: make known his deeds among the people.

Sing unto him, sing psalms unto him: talk ye of all his wondrous works.

Glory ye in his holy name: let the heart of them rejoice that seek the Lord.

Seek the Lord, and his strength: seek his face evermore.

Remember his marvelous works that he hath done; his wonders, and the judgments of his mouth.

PSALMS 105:1–5

Aging and Old Age

The poet Robert Browning wrote:

> Grow old along with me!
> The best is yet to be.
> The last of life, for which the first was made.
> Our times are in his hand.

But too often not even the finest of poets can offer the much needed sense of peace and acceptance when we face the very real facts of aging and old age, whether for ourselves, or for those we love.

But if we turn to the Holy Scriptures, we begin to understand that our fears have been groundless. There are compensations for growing older. The Word of God tells us that it also means growing wiser, becoming more knowledgeable, acquiring understanding of ourselves and of those we love.

Growing older is obviously part of God's Master Plan for us, and we know that in His wisdom, He has reason for all He does. The Bible tells us:

> With the ancient is wisdom; and in length of days understanding.
>
> JOB 12:12

> Remember the days of old, consider the years of many generations: ask thy father, and he will show thee; thy elders, and they will tell thee.
>
> DEUTERONOMY 32:7

19

Old age is meant to be respected. It is the time when knowledge, often gleaned with pain and garnered through suffering, can be passed on to those younger. Wouldn't it be wonderful if some of what we know can save those younger than us from tribulation?

Little by little, the order of God's World becomes more evident. We are His conduits, meant to pass on to those who follow us all that we can:

> O God, thou hast taught me from my youth: and hitherto have I declared thy wondrous works.
>
> Now also when I am old and gray-headed, O God, forsake me not; until I have showed thy strength unto this generation, and thy power to every one that is to come.
>
> PSALMS 71:17–18

> The days of our years are threescore years and ten; and if by reason of strength they be fourscore years, yet is their strength labor and sorrow; for it is soon cut off, and we fly away.
>
> Who knoweth the power of thine anger? Even according to thy fear, so is thy wrath.
>
> So teach us to number our days, that we may apply our hearts unto wisdom.
>
> PSALMS 90:10–12

Too often, age is associated with increasing weakness and debility. But this is not often the case. Many go on with great fortitude. Let us pray to the Lord that He keep us and those we love hale, even as we grow older:

> And Moses was a hundred and twenty years old when he died: his eye was not dim, nor his natural force abated.
>
> DEUTERONOMY 34:7

> And there arose not a prophet since in Israel like unto Moses, whom the Lord knew face to face.

In all the signs and the wonders, which the Lord sent him to do in the land of Egypt to Pharaoh, and to all his servants, and to all his land.

And in all that mighty hand, and in all the great terror which Moses showed in the sight of all Israel.

DEUTERONOMY 34:10–12

Aging, then, does not necessarily have to mean a time of *less,* but may even be a time of *more,* a time of greater spiritual strength.

As we grow older, we also grow more thoughtful. We have thought about God's only Son; we have thought about His sacrifice; we have thought about Him as our Redeemer. Others may marvel at our strength, our ability to do many physical things, but we know where that strength comes from:

I am as a wonder unto many; but thou art my strong refuge.

Let my mouth be filled with thy praise and with thy honor all the day.

Cast me not off in the time of old age; forsake me not when my strength faileth.

PSALMS 71:7–9

Old age should not be looked upon as a time of sadness or unhappiness. It is a time of opportunity, a time to give more thought to the meaning of our lives, a time to think constructively of the years we have ahead of us.

We have so much to do—to be worthy of our Saviour. The Word of God tells us that God granted long years to many of His children:

And Sarah was a hundred and seven and twenty years old: these were the years of the life of Sarah.

GENESIS 23:1

And Abraham was old, and well stricken in age: and the Lord had blessed Abraham in all things.

GENESIS 24:1

And these are the days of the years of Abraham's life which he lived, a hundred threescore and fifteen years.

Then Abraham gave up the ghost, and died in a good old age, an old man, and full of years; and was gathered to his people.

GENESIS 25:7–8

And these are the years of the life of Ishmael, a hundred and thirty and seven years: and he gave up the ghost and died; and was gathered unto his people.

GENESIS 25:17

Now, we know that God does not behave casually or carelessly. Long years are given for a reason; there is a purpose to all our lives.

The blessing of a long life can be used fruitfully. After years of rushing about, of never having time enough to do all the things we have always wanted to do, God has given us the gift of more time, and we can use these wonderful years by accepting God's Will every day.

The older we grow, the more we realize that He knows what is best for us.

As we grow older, our Saviour helps us to understand that He and His Father really do know what is best for us. With this understanding, we become aware of more spiritual needs:

Therefore I say unto you, Take no thought for your life, what ye shall eat, or what ye shall drink; nor yet for your body, what ye shall put on. Is not the life more than meat, and the body than raiment?

Behold the fowls of the air: for they sow not, neither do they reap, nor gather into barns; yet your heavenly Father feedeth them. Are ye not much better than they?

MATTHEW 6:25–26

It is not for us to decide the length of our years. Have you ever heard anyone say, "Well, I've lived too long"? But when we read of the many years given to Adam and Enoch and Methuselah, we begin to understand how foolish those words sound.

The purpose of longevity may not be clear to you, but you can be sure there is a purpose. Use God's blessing of a long life to be a source of loving kindness and spiritual aid to those you love:

> And Adam lived a hundred and thirty years, and begat a son in his own likeness, after his image; and called his name Seth:
> And the days of Adam after he had begotten Seth were eight hundred years: and he begat sons and daughters:
> And all the days that Adam lived were nine hundred and thirty years: and he died.
>
> GENESIS 5:3–5

> And Enoch lived sixty and five years, and begat Methuselah:
> And Enoch walked with God after he begat Methuselah three hundred years, and begat sons and daughters:
> And all the days of Enoch were three hundred sixty and five years:
> And Enoch walked with God: and he was not; for God took him.
>
> GENESIS 5:21–24

> Through faith also Sarah herself received strength to conceive seed, and was delivered of a child when she was past age, because she judged him faithful who had promised.
>
> HEBREWS 11:11

The Bible is filled with passages indicating concern for all of us as we grow older. And as the years pass, we, in turn, grow more concerned for our own spiritual welfare. Few of us can find the words to express these feelings properly, but if we turn to the Book of Psalms we gain solace, as we read:

> Remember, O Lord, thy tender mercies and thy loving-kindnesses; for they have been ever of old.
> Remember not the sins of my youth, nor my transgressions: according to thy mercy remember thou me for thy goodness' sake, O Lord.
>
> PSALMS 25:6–7

> For a thousand years in thy sight are but yesterday when it is past, and as a watch in the night.
>
> PSALMS 90:4

Sometimes we are puzzled. It seems as though one minute we are young and active, and the very next, our youth is gone:

> Thou carriest them away as with a flood; they are as a sleep: in the morning they are like grass which groweth up.
> In the morning it flourisheth, and groweth up; in the evening it is cut down, and withereth.
>
> PSALMS 90:5–6

But even as the years pass, our spiritual sight grows sharper. As we love our Lord and our Saviour, we begin to understand that They offer us our long life as a preface to our eventual salvation:

> Because he hath set his love upon me, therefore will I deliver him: I will set him on high, because he hath known my name.
> He shall call upon me, and I will answer him: I will be with him in trouble; I will deliver him, and honor him.
> With long life will I satisfy him, and show him my salvation.
>
> PSALMS 91:14–16

Remember that the quality of our lives is truly more important than the quantity. Long years are a great gift given to us by the One on High; don't waste His blessing:

> If a man beget a hundred children, and live many years, so that the days of his years be many, and his soul be not filled with good, and also that he have no burial; I say, that an untimely birth is better than he.
>
> For he cometh in with vanity, and departeth in darkness, and his name shall be covered with darkness.
>
> Moreover he hath not seen the sun, nor known any thing: this hath more rest than the other.
>
> Yea, though he live a thousand years twice told, yet hath he seen no good: do not all go to one place?
>
> ECCLESIASTES 6:3–6

> Wherefore I perceive that there is nothing better, than that a man should rejoice in his own works; for that is his portion: for who shall bring him to see what shall be after him?
>
> ECCLESIASTES 3:22

With every day that passes, we are that much older. We hope for a long life, and we will enjoy our own old age a great deal more if we know that in the past we always treated older people with the respect due their years

> Honor thy father and thy mother: that thy days may be long upon the land which the Lord thy God giveth thee.
>
> EXODUS 20:12

Alcoholism
and Addiction

In ancient times, many people believed that a person could be possessed by the Devil. Today, there are devils of a different sort that can lay waste a body and destroy a soul.

An uncontrollable craving for alcohol, a terrible addiction to drugs—these are the destructive forces that many of us battle with every day of our lives.

But why battle alone? The Word of God offers proof that help is waiting for you—just ask for it:

> Behold, the Lord's hand is not shortened, that it cannot save; neither his ear heavy, that it cannot hear.
>
> ISAIAH 59:1

Today, many people say, "No one understands what I'm contending with. Life is difficult in the twentieth century." They give modern times as the reason for their alcoholism or drug addiction.

But the Word of God shows us that this is a poor excuse. As the Bible indicates, this is not a problem of the times, but a problem of an afflicted spirit:

> Wine is a mocker, strong drink is raging: and whosoever is deceived thereby is not wise.
>
> PROVERBS 20:1

> Who hath woe? Who hath sorrow? Who hath contentions? Who hath babbling? Who hath wounds without cause? Who hath redness of eyes?

They that tarry long at the wine; they that go to seek mixed wine.

Look not upon the wine when it is red, when it giveth his color in the cup, when it moveth itself aright.

At the last it biteth like a serpent, and stingeth like an adder.

Thine eyes shall behold strange women, and thine heart shall utter perverse things.

Yea, thou shalt be as he that lieth down in the midst of the sea, or as he that lieth upon the top of a mast.

They have stricken me, shalt thou say, and I was not sick; they have beaten me, and I felt it not: when shall I awake? I will seek it yet again.

PROVERBS 23:29–35

As the Bible tells us, one of the great dangers of an addiction to alcohol or to drugs is that we may be unaware of the evil we commit while under the influence of strong drink or even stronger drugs.

When we're sober, and in a proper frame of mind, we are careful not to hurt the ones we love. Even as we try to rid ourselves of dangerous habits, we must also pray that we cause no additional pain to those around us:

And the firstborn said unto the younger, Our father is old, and there is not a man in the earth to come unto us after the manner of all the earth:

Come, let us make our father drink wine, and we will lie with him, that we may preserve seed of our father.

And they made their father drink wine that night: and the firstborn went in, and lay with her father; and he perceived not when she lay down, nor when she arose.

GENESIS 19:31–33

Sometimes, it seems impossible to continue the struggle against alcohol, drugs, or any destructive addiction. How can we go on? We are too weak!

But our weakness is no secret to our Saviour. It is faith in His strength that can help us in our battle:

> And he said unto me, My grace is sufficient for thee: for my strength is made perfect in weakness. Most gladly therefore will I rather glory in my infirmities, that the power of my Christ may rest upon me.
>
> II CORINTHIANS 12:9

All of us need all the help we can get. We go to doctors and to organizations that help those who suffer from addictions. Let us also pay special attention to His Word, and unburden ourselves as we repeat the Psalms:

> Save me, O God; for the waters are come in unto my soul.
> I sink in deep mire, where there is no standing: I am come into deep waters, where the floods overflow me.
> I am weary of my crying: my throat is dried: mine eyes fail while I wait for my God.
> They that hate me without a cause are more than the hairs of mine head: they that would destroy me, being mine enemies wrongfully, are mighty: then I restored that which I took not away.
> O God, thou knowest my foolishness; and my sins are not hid from thee.
>
> PSALMS 69:1–5

> Make haste, O God, to deliver me; make haste to help me, O Lord.
> Let them be ashamed and confounded that seek after my soul: let them be turned backward, and put to confusion, that desire my hurt.
> Let them be turned back for a reward of their shame that say, Aha, aha.
> Let all those that seek thee rejoice and be glad in thee: and let such as love thy salvation say continually, Let God be magnified.

But I am poor and needy: make haste unto me, O God: thou art my help and my deliverer; O Lord, make no tarrying.

PSALMS 70:1-5

Is there a way out of the mire of alcoholism? Can one step away from the fearsome trap of addiction? Nothing is impossible for those who believe, and who have faith in God and His Son.

You must live with both hope and patience in your heart. It took more than one day for you to become addicted, and it will take more than one day for you to be cured.

Go to our Lord as trustingly as a small child goes to his father, and our Heavenly Father will help you:

I waited patiently for the Lord; and he inclined unto me, and heard my cry.

He brought me up also out of a horrible pit, out of the miry clay, and set my feet upon a rock, and established my goings.

And he hath put a new song in my mouth, even praise unto our God: many shall see it, and fear, and shall trust in the Lord.

PSALMS 40:1-3

Even in your moment of great despair, the Scriptures convince us that we have many wonderful things to look forward to. Here are some comforting words that assure us of God's love:

For the Lord thy God bringeth thee into a good land, a land of brooks of water, of fountains and depths that spring out of valleys and hills;

A land of wheat, and barley, and vines, and fig trees, and pomegranates; a land of oil olive, and honey;

A land wherein thou shalt eat bread without scarceness, thou shalt not lack any thing in it; a land whose stones are iron, and out of whose hills thou mayest dig brass.

When thou hast eaten and art full, then thou shalt bless the Lord thy God for the good land which he hath given thee.

DEUTERONOMY 8:7–10

Our Saviour wants us to come to Him. Stress or anxiety may be among the causes of our addiction, but as we learn to rely on His strength, our anxious moments diminish, and so do our needs for either alcohol or drugs. We have grown stronger thanks to His love:

And he gave some, apostles; and some, prophets; and some, evangelists; and some, pastors and teachers;

For the perfecting of the saints, for the work of the ministry, for the edifying of the body of Christ:

Till we all come in the unity of the faith, and of the knowledge of the Son of God, unto a perfect man, unto the meacure of the stature of the fullness of Christ:

That we henceforth be no more children, tossed to and fro, and carried about with every wind of doctrine, by the sleight of men, and cunning craftiness, whereby they lie in wait to deceive;

But speaking the truth in love, may grow up into him in all things, which is the head, even Christ:

From whom the whole body fitly joined together and compacted by that which every joint supplieth, according to the effectual working in the measure of every part, maketh increase of the body unto the edifying of itself in love.

EPHESIANS 4:11–16

We were in terrible danger, but we were saved. It is well to remember the danger that has past, and to use it as an example for the future.

But most important, we should remember that it was the Holy Spirit that saved us:

See then that ye walk circumspectly, not as fools, but as wise,

Redeeming the time, because the days are evil.

Wherefore be ye not unwise, but understanding what the will of the Lord is.

And be not drunk with wine, wherein is excess; but be filled with the Spirit.

EPHESIANS 5:15–18

Do we thank each other for small kindnesses, slight favors? How much more important, then, to give abundant thanks now that we have been rescued:

Speaking to yourselves in psalms and hymns and spiritual songs, singing and making melody in your heart to the Lord;

Giving thanks always for all things unto God and the Father in the name of our Lord Jesus Christ;

Submitting yourselves one to another in the fear of God.

EPHESIANS 5:19–21

Beware that thou forget not the Lord thy God, in not keeping his commandments, and his judgments, and his statutes, which I command thee this day:

Lest when thou hast eaten and art full, and hast built goodly houses, and dwelt therein;

And when thy herds and thy flocks multiply, and thy silver and thy gold is multiplied, and all that thou hast is multiplied;

Then thine heart be lifted up, and thou forget the Lord thy God, which brought thee forth out of the land of Egypt, from the house of bondage;

Who led thee through that great and terrible wilderness, wherein were fiery serpents, and scorpions, and drought, where there was no water; who brought thee forth water out of the rock of flint;

Who fed thee in the wilderness with manna, which thy fathers knew not, that he might humble thee, and that he might prove thee, to do thee good at thy latter end;

And thou say in thine heart, My power and the might of mine hand hath gotten me this wealth.

But thou shalt remember the Lord thy God: for it is he that giveth thee power to get wealth, that he may establish his covenant which he sware unto thy fathers, as it is this day.

DEUTERONOMY 8:11–18

Anger and Resentment

Do you find yourself often in the grip of misplaced anger? Your resentment may be based more on fancy than on fact, and these bitter feelings are both wasteful and damaging.

There are times, of course, when all of us are moved to anger—justifiably so—but then there are those other, terrible times, when we lash out in a fury at those who have done nothing to deserve our rage.

The worst of it is when we rail at people we love; we know we're being unjust, but yet, we can't seem to control ourselves.

What can we do to check these wild outbursts? We can go to God's Inspired Word, and look to it for guidance:

> Be not hasty in thy spirit to be angry: for anger resteth in the bosom of fools.
>
> ECCLESIASTES 7:9

> He that hath no rule over his own spirit is like a city that is broken down, and without walls.
>
> PROVERBS 25:28

> An angry man stirreth up strife, and a furious man aboundeth in transgression.
>
> PROVERBS 29:22

> Be ye angry, and sin not: let not the sun go down upon your wrath.
>
> EPHESIANS 4:26

33

The Book tells us to restrain ourselves from anger, not only against our friends and loved ones, but even against our enemies. This is the way of Jesus Christ:

> Rejoice not when thine enemy falleth, and let not thine heart be glad when he stumbleth:
> Lest the Lord see it, and it displease him, and he turn away his wrath from him.
> Fret not thyself because of evil men, neither be thou envious at the wicked;
> For there shall be no reward to the evil man; the candle of the wicked shall be put out.
>
> PROVERBS 24:17–20

If we put our trust in the Holy Spirit, we will be led toward wisdom rather than foolishness. We are told that the wise man is a thoughtful man, and a thoughtful man knows that rage is not the best way to arrive at understanding:

> Scornful men bring a city into a snare: but wise men turn away wrath.
> If a wise man contendeth with a foolish man, whether he rage or laugh, there is no rest.
> The bloodthirsty hate the upright: but the just seek his soul.
>
> PROVERBS 29:8–10

What should we do, then, if we are so consumed with anger that we just don't know how to cope with our feelings and resentments?

What did the Lamb of God advise? As we hope for His forgiveness, and the forgiveness of our Father in Heaven, let us also hold out a hand of friendship and pardon:

> For if ye forgive men their trespasses, your heavenly Father will also forgive you:
> But if ye forgive not men their trespasses, neither will your Father forgive your trespasses.
>
> MATTHEW 6:14–15

A soft answer turneth away wrath: but grievous words stir up anger.

PROVERBS 15:1

The discretion of a man deferreth his anger; and it is his glory to pass over a transgression.

The king's wrath is as the roaring of a lion; but his favor is as dew upon the grass.

PROVERBS 19:11–12

Perhaps you know people who seem to be in a constant rage. They wear resentment like a black cloak constantly about them. If you have offered friendship, tried understanding, and nothing seems to help, the best thing for you to do may be a quiet withdrawal.

You can pray for these people and hope that they will be guided to the light by the Holy Spirit, but meanwhile, we are advised:

Make no friendship with an angry man; and with a furious man thou shalt not go;

Lest thou learn his ways, and get a snare to thy soul.

PROVERBS 22:24–25

For wrath killeth the foolish man, and envy slayeth the silly one.

JOB 5:2

Sometimes, though, you think to yourself that you are entitled to be angry by virtue of the fact that you are right and the other person is wrong.

But a person who is angry, even while he is right, is not as pleasing in the sight of our Lord, as a person who tempers his anger with forgiveness:

Take heed to yourselves: If thy brother trespass against thee, rebuke him; and if he repent, forgive him.

And if he trespass against thee seven times in a day,

and seven times in a day turn again to thee, saying, I repent; thou shalt forgive him.

LUKE 17:3-4

Anger and resentment are like fire. If allowed to rage on, unabated, it is we who will be consumed in the growing blaze.

If controlling rage is one of your problems, try substituting an even stronger feeling for your anger. Try love. This is the emotion our Saviour would so like us to share with Him:

A new commandment I give unto you, That ye love one another; as I have loved you, that ye also love one another.

By this shall all men know that ye are my disciples, if ye have love one to another.

JOHN 13:34-35

Owe no man any thing, but to love one another: for he that loveth another hath fulfilled the law.

ROMANS 13:8

Our Lord, Jesus Christ, wants us to be happy with Him. An angry, resentful person cannot possibly be happy; that's why God's Word tells us to love one another honestly, not pretending to enjoy the feeling of love if it isn't within our hearts:

Let love be without dissimulation. Abhor that which is evil; cleave to that which is good.

Be kindly affectioned one to another with brotherly love; in honor preferring one another.

ROMANS 12:9-10

Often, our growing awareness can restrain us from anger. We must be aware of the importance of our relationship to Jesus; we know what He would like us to do, how He would like us to behave. We want to be responsive to His words:

> Wherefore, my beloved brethren, let every man be swift to hear, slow to speak, slow to wrath:
> For the wrath of man worketh not the righteousness of God.
>
> JAMES 1:19–20

> He that is slow to anger is better than the mighty; and he that ruleth his spirit than he that taketh a city.
>
> PROVERBS 16:32

Bereavement

How can you face it? How can you face the loss of the person you loved so much? At first, there is the numbness—no feeling at all. But that's followed much too soon by strong feelings of pain, of deep sadness.

Is there anything, anything at all, that can ease your bereavement, comfort you for your loss?

You may be thinking, If only I had gone, and my loved one had stayed behind to mourn me, that would have been better.

Your sadness mounts, and mounts, until it is like a large wall surrounding you, completely cutting you off from the light of faith.

Deep mourning is understandable, and doctors advise that it is a good thing to go through for a brief period, it gives us time for some mental reconstruction.

However, mourning that continues without end indicates that our spirit, our very soul, has been affected, so much so that we have forgotten that our lives here are just a preface to the eternal life that awaits all those who believe in the sacrifice and redemption offered us by our beloved Saviour:

> Jesus cried and said, He that believeth on me, believeth not on me, but on him that sent me.
> And he that seeth me seeth him that sent me.
> I am come a light into the world, that whosoever believeth on me should not abide in darkness.
> And if any man hear my words, and believe not, I

judge him not: for I came not to judge the world, but to save the world.

He that rejecteth me, and receiveth not my words, hath one that judgeth him: the word that I have spoken, the same shall judge him in the last day.

For I have not spoken of myself; but the Father which sent me, he gave me a commandment, what I should say, and what I should speak.

And I know that his commandment is life everlasting: whatsoever I speak therefore, even as the Father said unto me, so I speak.

JOHN 12:44–50

The Scriptures make it clear that all through time people have wept for those they loved, and wished that they had been allowed to depart this world first. Remember King David's cries of pain:

And the king was much moved, and went up to the chamber over the gate, and wept: and as he went, thus he said, O my son Absalom! my son, my son Absalom! Would God I had died for thee, O Absalom, my son, my son!

II SAMUEL 18:33

The Book of Psalms also tells us that we are not the only ones to know such suffering:

How long wilt thou forget me, O Lord? For ever? How long wilt thou hide thy face from me?

How long shall I take counsel in my soul, having sorrow in my heart daily?

PSALMS 13:1–2

However, in time the spiritually healthy person is brought out of deep mourning by his own, strong, personal belief. He looks again to God, in whom he believes, and in whom he places his trust:

Why art thou cast down, O my soul? And why art thou disquieted within me? Hope thou in God: for I shall yet praise him, who is the health of my countenance, and my God.

PSALMS 42:11

I would seek unto God, and unto God would I commit my cause:
Which doeth great things and unsearchable; marvelous things without number:
Who giveth rain upon the earth, and sendeth waters upon the fields:
To set up on high those that be low; that those which mourn may be exalted to safety.

JOB 5:8–11

They that sow in tears shall reap in joy.
He that goeth forth and weepeth, bearing precious seed, shall doubtless come again with rejoicing, bringing his sheaves with him.

PSALMS 126:5–6

As one whom his mother comforteth, so will I comfort you; and ye shall be comforted in Jerusalem.

ISAIAH 66:13

It is well to remember, even as we mourn, that we are in truth mournful for ourselves. Has not the loved one we have lost gone on before us? And will we not meet again?

And Nathan departed unto his house. And the Lord struck the child that Uriah's wife bare unto David, and it was very sick.
David therefore besought God for the child; and David fasted, and went in, and lay all night upon the earth.
And the elders of his house arose, and went to him, to raise him up from the earth: but he would not, neither did he eat bread with them.
And it came to pass on the seventh day, that the child

died. And the servants of David feared to tell him that the child was dead: for they said, Behold, while the child was yet alive, we spake unto him, and he would not hearken unto our voice: how will he then vex himself, if we tell him that the child is dead?

But when David saw that his servants whispered, David perceived that the child was dead: therefore David said unto his servants, Is the child dead? And they said, He is dead.

Then David arose from the earth, and washed, and anointed himself, and changed his apparel, and came into the house of the Lord, and worshipped: then he came to his own house; and when he required, they set bread before him, and he did eat.

Then said his servants unto him, What thing is this that thou hast done? Thou didst fast and weep for the child while it was alive; but when the child was dead, thou didst rise and eat bread.

And he said, While the child was yet alive, I fasted and wept: for I said, Who can tell whether God will be gracious to me, that the child may live?

But now he is dead, wherefore should I fast? can I bring him back again? I shall go to him, but he shall not return to me.

II SAMUEL 12:15–23

But I would not have you be ignorant, brethren, concerning them which are asleep, that ye sorrow not, even as others which have no hope.

I THESSALONIANS 4:13

Blessed are they that mourn: for they shall be comforted.

MATTHEW 5:4

As time goes by, we gain measure after measure of spiritual comfort, it is like drinking swallow after swallow of cool water when we're extremely thirsty, and our throats are parched.

However, every day is not an unmitigated joy. Doubt still assails us. Try as we might, we cannot always be strong in our faith. And then we are reminded once again:

> Even in laughter the heart is sorrowful; and the end of that mirth is heaviness.
>
> PROVERBS 14:13

> Now it came to pass on a certain day, that he went into a ship with his disciples: and he said unto them, Let us go over unto the other side of the lake. And they launched forth.
>
> But as they sailed, he fell asleep: and there came down a storm of wind on the lake; and they were filled with water, and were in jeopardy.
>
> And they came to him, and awoke him, saying, Master, master, we perish. Then he arose, and rebuked the wind and the raging of the water: and they ceased, and there was a calm.
>
> And he said unto them, Where is your faith? And they being afraid wondered, saying one to another, What manner of man is this! for he commandeth even the winds and the water, and they obey him.
>
> LUKE 8:22–25

We know, then, that even though we are sad today, our sorrow is a passing thing, and in time we will be happy and together once again. Our Book tells us:

> And I saw a new heaven and a new earth: for the first heaven and the first earth were passed away; and there was no more sea.
>
> And I John saw the holy city, new Jerusalem, coming down from God out of heaven, prepared as a bride adorned for her husband.
>
> And I heard a great voice out of heaven saying, Behold, the tabernacle of God is with men, and he will dwell with them, and they shall be his people, and God himself shall be with them, and be their God.

And God shall wipe away all tears from their eyes; and there shall be no more death, neither sorrow, nor crying, neither shall there be any more pain: for the former things are passed away.

REVELATION 21:1–4

Sadness is a part of life; we have come to understand that. The order of God's universe is such, that in time we come to know many things, many emotions. But loving God and Jesus, and being loved by Them, can give us the security of knowing that we are with Them, and that They want us to feel comforted:

The Lord bless thee, and keep thee:
The Lord make his face shine upon thee, and be gracious unto thee:
The Lord lift up his countenance upon thee, and give thee peace.

NUMBERS 6:24–26

Confusion and Doubt

Even the strongest believer is beset with confusion, and many of us are faced with doubts from time to time.

There is confusion about the path to take, and doubt about the best way to arrive at a goal. Many of us know a feeling of weakness when faced with seemingly insurmountable difficulties.

The worst time, of course, is when our confusions and doubts are caused by spiritual wavering; however, it is good to know that the most faithful were attacked by doubt. Doubt is often a testing of our faith, and when we overcome it, we arrive at a great spiritual happiness.

Admit to your doubts, because, as the poet George MacDonald wrote:

> The man that feareth, Lord, to doubt,
> In that fear doubteth Thee.

Recognizing your doubts is the first step toward overcoming them. God and His Son want us to accept Them in our minds as well as in our hearts, and as Alfred, Lord Tennyson said,

> There lives more faith in honest doubt,
> Believe me, than in half the creeds.

Don't be afraid, then, when experiencing confusion and doubt; use them while working your way toward a stronger faith. And don't be fearful that you will be deserted as you travel through the maze of problems that face you, because the Book says:

> . . . I will not fail thee, nor forsake thee.
>
> JOSHUA 1:5

> And thine ears shall hear a word behind thee, saying, This is the way, walk ye in it, when ye turn to the right hand, and when ye turn to the left.
>
> ISAIAH 30:21

Many a person has been rescued from the most paralyzing doubts, the most fearful confusions of the soul, when reading:

> Then spake Jesus again unto them, saying, I am the light of the world: he that followeth me shall not walk in darkness, but shall have the light of life.
>
> JOHN 8:12

Much is possible if you believe, and perhaps you yearn to believe without asking, "Why?" But think of the way children go to their fathers and mothers with their questions. Just as their parents try to answer them, so our Heavenly Father tries to answer you.

Sometimes, the answer lies in the fact that the ways of God are wonderful, and that nothing is impossible if He wishes it to be so:

> For verily I say unto you, That whosoever shall say unto this mountain, Be thou removed, and be thou cast into the sea; and shall not doubt in his heart, but shall believe that those things which he saith shall come to pass; he shall have whatsoever he saith.
>
> Therefore I say unto you, What things soever ye desire, when ye pray, believe that ye receive them, and ye shall have them.
>
> MARK 11:23–24

The Holy Scriptures are full of God's miracles; as we study them, they assuage our doubts. We begin to understand that if God can do so very much, He can, of course, help us:

> And the Lord said unto Joshua, See, I have given into thine hand Jericho, and the king thereof, and the mighty men of valor.
> And ye shall compass the city, all ye men of war, and go round about the city once. Thus shalt thou do six days.
> And seven priests shall bear before the ark seven trumpets of rams' horns: and the seventh day ye shall compass the city seven times, and the priests shall blow with the trumpets.
> And it shall come to pass, that when they make a long blast with the ram's horn, and when ye hear the sound of the trumpet, all the people shall shout with a great shout; and the wall of the city shall fall down flat, and the people shall ascend up every man straight before him.
>
> JOSHUA 6:2–5

> So the people shouted when the priests blew with the trumpets: and it came to pass, when the people heard the sound of the trumpet, and the people shouted with a great shout, that the wall fell down flat, so that the people went up into the city, every man straight before him, and they took the city.
>
> JOSHUA 6:20

> Another parable put he forth unto them, saying, The kingdom of heaven is like to a grain of mustard seed, which a man took, and sowed in his field:
> Which indeed is the least of all seeds: but when it is grown, it is the greatest among herbs, and becometh a tree, so that the birds of the air come and lodge in the branches thereof.
>
> MATTHEW 13:31–32

Faith and belief can help us overcome confusion and doubt. It is not always necessary to see everything with our eyes; sometimes we must see through the even clearer eyes our belief in the Saviour:

> Now faith is the substance of things hoped for, the evidence of things not seen.
>
> HEBREWS 11:1

> A man's heart deviseth his way: but the Lord directeth his steps.
>
> PROVERBS 16:9

Sometimes we find ourselves wandering about as though we were in a dark forest. Which way to turn? How shall we proceed? If you feel that way, stop, relax, and put yourself in the hands of our Lord. He will take care of you:

> He shall feed his flock like a shepherd: he shall gather the lambs with his arm, and carry them in his bosom, and shall gently lead those that are with young.
>
> ISAIAH 40:11

> For I am persuaded, that neither death, nor life, nor angels, nor principalities, nor powers, nor things present, nor things to come,
> Nor height, nor depth, nor any other creature, shall be able to separate us from the love of God, which is in Christ Jesus our Lord.
>
> ROMANS 8:38–39

The next time you are assailed by doubt, remember the words of Jesus to Nicodemus:

> Verily, verily, I say unto thee, We speak that we do know, and testify that we have seen; and ye receive not our witness.

> If I have told you earthly things, and ye believe not,
> how shall ye believe, if I tell you of heavenly things?
>
> JOHN 3:11–12

If you have rid yourself of doubts, offer the light of your faith in Jesus Christ to others:

> No man, when he hath lighted a candle, covereth it with a vessel, or putteth it under a bed; but setteth it on a candlestick, that they which enter in may see the light.
> For nothing is secret, that shall not be made manifest; neither any thing hid, that shall not be known and come abroad.
>
> LUKE 8:16–17

Through the centuries, many have testified as to the help they have received from Christ when they have come to Him with heartfelt prayers. This comes as no surprise to those who have read:

> For I know the thoughts that I think toward you, saith the Lord, thoughts of peace, and not of evil, to give you an expected end.
> Then shall ye call upon me, and ye shall go and pray unto me, and I will hearken unto you.
> And ye shall seek me, and find me, when ye shall search for me with all your heart.
>
> JEREMIAH 29:11–13

As belief replaces doubt, we can understand the calm sureness of Paul, when he spoke to the Athenians:

> Then Paul stood in the midst of Mars' hill, and said, Ye men of Athens, I perceive that in all things ye are too superstitious.
> For as I passed by, and beheld your devotions, I found an altar with this inscription, TO THE UNKNOWN GOD. Whom therefore ye ignorantly worship, him declare I unto you.

God that made the world and all things therein, seeing that he is Lord of heaven and earth, dwelleth not in temples made with hands;

Neither is worshipped with men's hands, as though he needed any thing, seeing he giveth to all life, and breath, and all things;

And hath made of one blood all nations of men for to dwell on all the face of the earth, and hath determined the times before appointed, and the bounds of their habitation;

That they should seek the Lord, if haply they might feel after him, and find him, though he be not far from every one of us:

For in him we live, and move, and have our being; as certain also of your own poets have said, For we are also his offspring.

ACTS 17:22–38

At last the search is ended, our souls are at peace and comforted. We have come to Him. It cannot be otherwise, when we read:

Verily, verily, I say unto you, He that believeth on me hath everlasting life.

I am that bread of life.

Your fathers did eat manna in the wilderness, and are dead.

This is the bread which cometh down from heaven, that a man may eat thereof, and not die.

I am the living bread which came down from heaven; if any man eat of this bread, he shall live for ever: and the bread that I will give is my flesh, which I will give for the life of the world.

JOHN 6:47–51

Do not berate yourself if it has taken you awhile to accept without seeing. In time, as your faith grows stronger, your confusions and doubts will become weaker, and then you will be one of the blessed whom Jesus spoke about:

But Thomas, one of the twelve, called Didymus, was not with them when Jesus came.

The other disciples therefore said unto him, We have seen the Lord. But he said unto them, Except I shall see in his hands the print of the nails, and put my finger into the print of the nails, and thrust my hand into his side, I will not believe.

And after eight days again his disciples were within, and Thomas with them: then came Jesus, the doors being shut, and stood in the midst, and said, Peace be unto you.

Then saith he to Thomas, Reach hither thy finger, and behold my hands; and reach hither thy hand, and thrust it into my side; and be not faithless, but believing.

And Thomas answered and said unto him, My Lord and my God.

Jesus saith unto him, Thomas, because thou hast seen me, thou hast believed: blessed are they that have not seen, and yet have believed.

JOHN 20:24–29

Crises

If only life were simple and easy! It would be wonderful if we could spend each day working, caring for one another, enjoying the gift of life that God has given to us. But life is never that simple—not for anyone.

There are wonderful days, days that we wish would last, but the sunny days are followed by cloudy ones. We have problems, troubles, worries.

Sometimes, we see little mishaps and regard them as large crises—nightmares! But there are other times when we don't exaggerate our problems, and we wonder how we can get through the very next day.

We talk about our problems to our friends, our family. Talking things out helps somewhat, but when things get really bad, we know that it is God who must help us find the courage to see things through.

And as we turn to Jesus for compassion, we look to God for fortitude:

> And the Lord, he it is that doth go before thee; he will be with thee, he will not fail thee, neither forsake thee: fear not, neither be dismayed.
>
> DEUTERONOMY 31:8

The Holy Scriptures tell us of some of God's other children. They were captured by an enemy and taken to a foreign land; they were held in bondage; they were slaves of a strange king. There were times when they were sure that

they had been forgotten. But God didn't forget them, nor
has He forgotten you:

> And the Lord spake unto Moses, Go unto Pharaoh,
> and say unto him, Thus saith the Lord, Let my people
> go, that they may serve me.
>
> EXODUS 8:1

> And the Lord went before them by day in a pillar of a
> cloud, to lead them the way; and by night in a pillar of
> fire, to give them light; to go by day and night:
> He took not away the pillar of the cloud by day, nor
> the pillar of fire by night, from before the people.
>
> EXODUS 13:21–22

Are we being tested by our troubles? Perhaps. Many of
the crises we face seem to wrench at our hearts, our souls.

At the worst time in our lives we must remember the
words of Jesus Christ, who promised us the greatest comfort of all:

> But the Comforter, which is the Holy Ghost, whom
> the Father will send in my name, he shall teach you all
> things, and bring all things to your remembrance, what-
> soever I have said unto you.
>
> JOHN 14:26

We must learn to accept the fact that our lives were not
meant to be perfect here on earth. As we work toward our
salvation, we come to understand that all of us are faced
with a great variety of problems that change throughout
the years:

> Although affliction cometh not forth of the dust, nei-
> ther doth trouble spring out of the ground;
> Yet man is born unto trouble, as the sparks fly upward.
>
> JOB 5:6–7

The best thing you can do when faced with a crisis is to keep reminding yourself that you are not alone. Say it in the morning, say it in the evening, say it as you turn to God and ask Him for help. Understand that even though your problems may continue, God will give you the inner spiritual reserves to live with them.

Don't say, "I can do this by myself. I don't need any help." There is nothing weak in turning to God:

> This poor man cried, and the Lord heard him, and saved him out of all his troubles.
>
> PSALMS 34:6

> Many are the afflictions of the righteous: but the Lord delivereth him out of them all.
>
> PSALMS 34:19

> Lord, how are they increased that trouble me! Many are they that rise up against me.
>
> Many there be which say of my soul, There is no help for him in God. Selah.
>
> But thou, O Lord, art a shield for me; my glory, and the lifter up of mine head.
>
> I cried unto the Lord with my voice, and he heard me out of his holy hill. Selah.
>
> I laid me down and slept; I awaked; for the Lord sustained me.
>
> I will not be afraid of ten thousands of people, that have set themselves against me round about.
>
> PSALMS 3:1–6

The feeling that no one cares about what happens to you during a crisis can be a very destructive one. Look around you! Your family, your friends, many of them do care a great deal, even though their ability to help you may be limited.

However, God also cares, and His ability is never limited. Turn to Him with your sincere prayers, and ask Him to help you find a solution to your problems:

> Turn thee unto me, and have mercy upon me; for I am desolate and afflicted.
>
> The troubles of my heart are enlarged: O bring thou me out of my distresses.
>
> PSALMS 25:16–17

> I will lift up mine eyes unto the hills, from whence cometh my help.
>
> My help cometh from the Lord, which made heaven and earth.
>
> He will not suffer thy foot to be moved: he that keepeth thee will not slumber.
>
> Behold, he that keepeth Israel shall neither slumber nor sleep.
>
> The Lord is thy keeper: the Lord is thy shade upon thy right hand.
>
> The sun shall not smite thee by day, nor the moon by night.
>
> The Lord shall preserve thee from all evil: he shall preserve thy soul.
>
> The Lord shall preserve thy going out and thy coming in from this time forth, and even for evermore.
>
> PSALMS 121:1–8

Do you feel that lack of courage? Perhaps you are disappointed in yourself for not being braver, not having more fortitude when you are in the midst of a crisis. Take comfort in the knowledge that everyone has moments of weakness; it is a natural part of being a man.

God does not expect us always to stand without fear. Remember that even Jesus' disciple Peter was once so fearful that he denied our Lord three times in one night.

The Word of God contains many prayers by those who knew fear, and who knew that their ultimate strength had to come from God:

Fearfulness and trembling are come upon me, and homor hath overwhelmed me.

And I said, Oh that I had wings like a dove! For then would I fly away, and be at rest.

PSALMS 55:5–6

If thou faint in the day of adversity, thy strength is small.

PROVERBS 24:10

When facing a large crisis, it is usually best not to dash about, searching for solutions in many directions.

Quiet your spirit, and turn your thoughts to God:

For thus saith the Lord God, the Holy One of Israel; In returning and rest shall ye be saved; in quietness and in confidence shall be your strength: and ye would not.

ISAIAH 30:15

Seek ye the Lord while he may be found, call ye upon him while he is near.

ISAIAH 55:6

The Bible tells us that we must all be soldiers with Christ. As soldiers, we gain strength when we remember once again whom we are following: Jesus Christ:

I can do all things through Christ which strengtheneth me.

PHILIPPIANS 4:13

There is no danger so grave, no problem so serious, that cannot be helped with the intervention of God. No one is slighting the enemies you face, but just remember that Daniel was saved by God's Hand in the person of an angel, when he was thrown into the den of lions:

Then the king commanded, and they brought Daniel, and cast him into the den of lions. Now the king spake and said unto Daniel, Thy God whom thou servest continually, he will deliver thee.

And a stone was brought, and laid upon the mouth of the den; and the king sealed it with his own signet, and with the signet of his lords; that the purpose might not be changed concerning Daniel.

Then the king went to his palace, and passed the night fasting: neither were instruments of music brought before him: and his sleep went from him.

Then the king arose very early in the morning, and went in haste unto the den of lions.

And when he came to the den, he cried with a lamentable voice unto Daniel: and the king spake and said to Daniel, O Daniel, servant of the living God, is thy God, whom thou servest continually, able to deliver thee from the lions?

Then said Daniel unto the king, O king, live for ever.

My God hath sent his angel, and hath shut the lions' mouths, that they have not hurt me: forasmuch as before him innocency was found in me; and also before thee, O king, have I done no hurt.

Then was the king exceeding glad for him, and commanded that they should take Daniel up out of the den. So Daniel was taken up out of the den, and no manner of hurt was found upon him, because he believed in his God.

DANIEL 6:16–23

O Lord, thou art my God; I will exalt thee, I will praise thy name; for thou hast done wonderful things; thy counsels of old are faithfulness and truth.

ISAIAH 25:1

Today is bad, but tomorrow can, and will, be better. As, in the past, your problems were solved, the crisis you face now will also pass away.

Our Saviour wants us to be joyful, just as our Father in Heaven wants us to find happiness in the world He created for us:

How beautiful upon the mountains are the feet of him that bringeth good tidings, that publisheth peace; that bringeth good tidings of good, that publisheth salvation; that saith unto Zion, Thy God reigneth!

ISAIAH 52:7

Notwithstanding the Lord stood with me, and strengthened me; that by me the preaching might be fully known, and that all the Gentiles might hear: and I was delivered out of the mouth of the lion.

II TIMOTHY 4:17

Death and Dying

We are all like children when we think of death, or face the thought of dying. Like children, we are afraid of the dark, of a future we cannot see.

But, as children are comforted by loving parents, so we can gain comfort from the promise of eternity that was given to us by God.

Our Lord has stretched out His Hand to us, He gave us His Son and He allowed that Son to sacrifice for us. As we come to God through the Saviour, we repent our sins, and we are saved—saved, born again, and ready for life eternal.

Jesus Christ sacrificed for us—for you, for all of us—and it is this symbol of the sacrifice that the preacher and poet, John Donne, celebrated, when he wrote:

> He was the Word, that spake it;
> He took the bread and brake it;
> And what that Word did make it,
> I do believe and take it.

Are you prepared to accept that sacrifice? If you are, and if you come to Jesus Christ, sorry for your sins, and understanding that you can be saved through Him, then death need not be a fearful element in your life. You can agree with John Donne, who further wrote:

> Death, be not proud, though some have called thee
> Mighty and dreadful, for thou art not so,

For those whom thou think'st thou doest overthrow,
Die not, poor Death; nor yet canst thou kill me.
One short sleep past, we wake eternally,
And death shall be no more; Death, thou shalt die!

Suddenly, the world looks wonderful once again! Our terrors are diminished, as we realize that our fears were groundless. Our God and His Son have us in Their loving care, and we begin to understand that this life is only the beginning. Death for those who are redeemed is merely the doorway that leads to Him.

The Bible tells us very clearly what our Saviour said:

> Jesus said unto her, I am the resurrection, and the life: he that believeth in me, though he were dead, yet shall he live:
> And whosoever liveth and believeth in me shall never die. Believest thou this?
>
> JOHN 11:25–26

> After two days will he revive us: in the third day he will raise us up, and we shall live in his sight.
>
> HOSEA 6:2

Perhaps you worry about your past; it hasn't been a blameless one. Even though you are penitent today, what about all the days that went before? Will there be room for you with Jesus? Read and remember His words:

> In my Father's house are many mansions: if it were not so, I would have told you. I go to prepare a place for you.
>
> JOHN 14:2

The Holy Word of God explains very clearly that only those who remain enmeshed in their sins, only those who have not come, with faith and love to Jesus, asking to be saved, need be frightened of death:

> O death, where is thy sting? O grave, where is thy victory?
>
> The sting of death is sin; and the strength of sin is the law.
>
> But thanks be to God, which giveth us victory through our Lord Jesus Christ.
>
> I CORINTHIANS 15:55–57

It has not been given to us to understand God's Plan, but we can accept it when we trust in Jesus' love, and realize that though our days are numbered here, they are numberless in eternity:

> Lord, make me to know mine end, and the measure of my days, what it is; that I may know how frail I am.
>
> PSALMS 39:4

> As for man, his days are as grass: as a flower of the field, so he flourisheth.
>
> For the wind passeth over it, and it is gone; and the place thereof shall know it no more.
>
> But the mercy of the Lord is from everlasting to everlasting upon them that fear him, and his righteousness unto children's children;
>
> To such as keep his covenant, and to those that remember his commandments to them.
>
> PSALMS 103:15–18

Our bodies are important to us here, of course, but it is our souls that contain the eternal truth of our love for Jesus Christ, and His love for us, and it is these shining souls that go on to God:

> Also when they shall be afraid of that which is high, and fears shall be in the way, and the almond tree shall flourish, and the grasshopper shall be a burden, and desire shall fail: because man goeth to his lone home, and the mourners go about the streets:

Or ever the silver cord be loosed, or the golden bowl be broken, or the pitcher be broken at the fountain, or the wheel broken at the cistern.

Then shall the dust return to the earth as it was: and the spirit shall return unto God who gave it.

ECCLESIASTES 12:5–7

Behold, I show you a mystery; We shall not all sleep, but we shall all be changed,

In a moment, in the twinkling of an eye, at the last trump: for the trumpet shall sound, and the dead shall be raised incorruptible, and we shall be changed.

I CORINTHIANS 15:51–52

When we think of the future—of the real, eternal future—we begin to understand how unimportant are all our acquisitions here on earth. They give us ease and comfort, true, but it is only those things that are within our hearts and souls that will travel with us on our eternal journey:

... Naked came I out of my mother's womb, and naked shall I return thither: the Lord gave, and the Lord hath taken away; blessed be the name of the Lord.

JOB 1:21

For we brought nothing into this world, and it is certain we can carry nothing out.

I TIMOTHY 6:7

When a day's work is finished, we are tired, and want to go home to rest. In the same way, when Jesus' work was finished on earth, He went home to His Father.

He has told us that when our life's work is over, we can go to our true home with Him:

These words spake Jesus, and lifted up his eyes to heaven, and said, Father, the hour is come; glorify thy Son that thy Son also may glorify thee:

As thou hast given him power over all flesh, that he should give eternal life to as many as thou hast given him.

And this is life eternal, that they might know thee the only true God, and Jesus Christ, whom thou hast sent.

I have glorified thee on earth: I have finished the work which thou gavest me to do.

And now, O Father, glorify thou me with thine own self with the glory which I had with thee before the world was.

JOHN 17:1–5

Jesus saith unto her, Touch me not; for I am not yet ascended to my Father: but go to my brethren, and say unto them, I ascend unto my Father, and your Father; and to my God, and your God.

JOHN 20:17

Not only does God's Word tell us that we shall join Jesus Christ, we are also given the blessed news that we shall be like Him whom we adore—without sin:

Beloved, now are we the sons of God, and it doth not yet appear what we shall be: but we know that, when he shall appear, we shall be like him; for we shall see him as he is.

I JOHN 3:2

While we are here, on earth, we cannot expect to understand the miracle of life everlasting; but in time, knowledge will surely be given to us all:

For now we see through a glass, darkly; but then face to face: now I know in part; but then shall I know even as also I am known.

I CORINTHIANS 13:12

Saying with a loud voice, Fear God, and give glory to him; for the hour of his judgment is come: and worship

him that made heaven, and earth, and the sea, and the
fountains of waters.

REVELATION 14:7

The end of life, then, is not only the end, but a beginning. How can we prepare for our future? By looking forward with faith, and serene belief in our Lord:

For I know that my Redeemer liveth, and that he
shall stand at the latter day upon the earth:
And though after my skin worms destroy this body, yet
in my flesh shall I see God.

JOB 19:25–26

The promise given to us is manifold and wonderful:
not only will we have a life eternal, but that life will be
free of the suffering that we know here on earth:

There the wicked cease from troubling; and there the
weary be at rest.

JOB 3:17

For I reckon that the sufferings of this present time
are not worthy to be compared with the glory which
shall be revealed in us.

ROMANS: 8:18

Verily, verily, I say unto you, The hour is coming, and
now is, when the dead shall hear the voice of the Son of
God: and they that hear shall live.

JOHN 5:25

The next time you are oppressed by thoughts of death
and dying, consult God's Holy Scriptures for comfort. His
promise of life eternal for those who believe in Him was
made many times, and recorded many times in the Bible:

For he that is dead is freed from sin.
Now if we be dead with Christ, we believe that we
shall also live with him:

Knowing that Christ being raised from the dead dieth no more; death hath no more dominion over him.

For in that he died, he died unto sin once: but in that he liveth, he liveth unto God.

Likewise reckon ye also yourselves to be dead indeed unto sin, but alive unto God through Jesus Christ our Lord.

ROMANS: 6:7–11

We've been told that if we listen to the Holy Spirit, and accept salvation through Jesus Christ, we shall abide with Him:

He that hath an ear, let him hear what the Spirit saith unto the churches: To him that overcometh will I give to eat of the tree of life, which is in the midst of the paradise of God.

REVELATION 2:7

For I am now ready to be offered, and the time of my departure is at hand.

I have fought a good fight, I have finished my course, I have kept the faith:

Henceforth there is laid up for me a crown of righteousness, which the Lord, the righteous judge, shall give me at that day: and not to me only, but unto all them also that love his appearing.

II TIMOTHY 4:6–8

Sometimes, it is in the middle of the dark night, when fear descends upon us—the unreasoning fear that the darkness of the night may engulf us forever. It is then time to sit up, turn on the light, and remember the loving words meant to rid us of sadness, gloom, and fear:

For God so loved the world, that he gave his only begotten Son, that whosoever believeth in him should not perish, but have everlasting life.

JOHN 3:16

If we are still looking for assurance, the Word of God tells us clearly that we will reap that which we have sown:

> And I heard a voice from heaven saying unto me, Write, Blessed are the dead which die in the Lord from henceforth: Yea, saith the Spirit, that they may rest from their labors; and their works do follow them.
>
> And I looked, and behold a white cloud, and upon the cloud one sat like unto the Son of man, having on his head a golden crown, and in his hand a sharp sickle.
>
> And another angel came out of the temple, crying with a loud voice to him that sat on the cloud, Thrust in thy sickle, and reap: for the time is come for thee to reap; for the harvest of the earth is ripe.
>
> REVELATION 14:13–15

Depression and Despair

There are times when our souls are filled with an oppressive disquiet. Occasionally, we can trace these moods of depression to a specific cause, but there are other times when we just cannot find the exact reason for our despair.

If we sit down and think, and try to remember what it is that has upset us so, we may realize that our depression is based on something unkind that we may have done to another. Our sin may loom large in our own mind, so large that we fear that our Saviour will never forgive us. Our faith trembles as we think that we will not be able to come to Him.

At such times, it is important to remember that God put His Son here on earth so that He could offer us the forgiveness we all need. Jesus Christ will not turn from you if you come to Him.

To cope with depression best, we must remember that life here on this earth was never intended to be always easy and simple. Why this is, we cannot know; we have not yet been made privy to God's purpose.

However, what we do know is that we can trust in God during our worst moments, and it is to Him we must turn, repeating the words of the psalmist:

> Hear my prayer, O Lord, and let my cry come unto thee.
> Hide not thy face from me in the day when I am in trouble; incline thine ear unto me: in the day when I call answer me speedily.

For my days are consumed like smoke, and my bones are burned as a hearth.

My heart is smitten, and withered like grass; so that I forget to eat my bread.

By reason of the voice of my groaning my bones cleave to my skin.

I am like a pelican of the wilderness: I am like an owl of the desert.

I watch, and am as a sparrow alone upon the house top.

Mine enemies reproach me all the day; and they are mad against me are sworn against me.

For I have eaten ashes like bread, and mingled my drink with weeping.

Because of thine indignation and thy wrath: for thou hast lifted me up, and cast me down.

My days are like a shadow that declineth; and I am withered like grass.

PSALMS 102:1–11

Your depression, your despair, is not unique. Even Jesus' disciples suffered from these feelings, and needed the reassurance of the Son of God, who said to them:

Let not your heart be troubled: ye believe in God, believe also in me.

JOHN 14:1

Just as a parent pities a child who weeps and is sad, so God pities us in our sadness:

Like as a father pitieth his children, so the Lord pitieth them that fear him.

For he knoweth our frame; he remembereth that we are dust.

PSALMS 103:13–14

It is the wish of our heavenly Father that we find happiness in this life:

Go thy way, eat thy bread with joy, and drink thy wine with a merry heart; for God now accepteth thy works.

ECCLESIASTES 9:7

When your days seem gray and meaningless, remember that loving God and Jesus, and obeying the commandments, can bring you from the darkest moods into the light:

If ye love me, keep my commandments.
And I will pray the Father, and he shall give you another Comforter, that he may abide with you for ever.

JOHN 14:15–16

If ye keep my commandments, ye shall abide in my love; even as I have kept my Father's commandments, and abide in his love.
These things have I spoken unto you, that my joy might remain in you, and that your joy might be full.

JOHN 15:10–11

Was there ever anyone more afflicted, and more depressed, than Job?

After this opened Job his mouth, and cursed his day.
And Job spake, and said,
Let the day perish wherein I was born, and the night in which it was said, There is a man child conceived.

JOB 3:1–3

Why is light given to a man whose way is hid, and whom God hath hedged in?
For my sighing cometh before I eat, and my roarings are poured out like the waters.
For the thing which I greatly feared is come upon me, and that which I was afraid of is come unto me.

I was not in safety, neither had I rest, neither was I
quiet; yet trouble came.

JOB 3:23-26

And after Job suffered much, God did bring an end to
his despair:

And the Lord turned the captivity of Job, when he
prayed for his friends: also the Lord gave Job twice as
much as he had before.

JOB 42:10

So the Lord blessed the latter end of Job more than
his beginning: for he had fourteen thousand sheep, and
six thousand camels, and a thousand yoke of oxen, and
a thousand she asses.
He had also seven sons and three daughters.

JOB 42:12-13

But more than the material goods of the world, Job ar-
rived at spiritual peace, the peace we all long for. To at-
tain it, keep reminding yourself that the feelings of despair you are now experiencing will end.

Remember, though you have sinned, if you repent,
your sins will be forgiven. You have hope for a better
tomorrow, because you are secure in the knowledge that
God loves you. It is God's plan that things will work out
for the best after a time:

And we know that all things work together for good
to them that love God, to them who are the called according to his purpose.

ROMANS 8:28

When men are cast down, then thou shalt say, There
is lifting up; and he shall save the humble person.

JOB 22:29

> Now the God of hope fill you with all joy and peace in believing, that ye may abound in hope, through the power of the Holy Ghost.
>
> ROMANS 15:13

The Shepherd who tends our Father's sheep knows how tired you are. He alone can understand the depths of your depression. Because He does understand, He wants to take your sad burden from you. Surely, so much love will lighten your feelings of despair:

> Come unto me, all ye that labor and are heavy laden, and I will give you rest.
>
> Take my yoke upon you, and learn of me; for I am meek and lowly in heart: and ye shall find rest unto your souls.
>
> For my yoke is easy, and my burden is light.
>
> MATTHEW 11:28–30

> The eyes of the Lord are upon the righteous, and his ears are open unto their cry.
>
> The face of the Lord is against them that do evil, to cut off the remembrance of them from the earth.
>
> The righteous cry, and the Lord heareth, and delivereth them out of all their troubles.
>
> PSALMS 34:15–17

Put an end to sadness, depression, and despair, because true happiness awaits the believer—now and ever after:

> Therefore they shall come and sing in the height of Zion, and shall flow together to the goodness of the Lord, for wheat, and for wine, and for oil, and for the young of the flock and of the herd: and their soul shall be as a watered garden; and they shall not sorrow any more at all.
>
> JEREMIAH 31:12

Do not let others contribute to your feelings of depression. If you can, take other people with you as you move from feelings of despair to those of contentment.

The Bible offers us passages of great joy, and reminds us of the beauties of God's earth. Open your eyes wide, and look at this wondrous world God has made for you:

> Rejoice, and be exceeding glad: for great is your reward in heaven: for so persecuted they the prophets which were before you.
>
> MATTHEW 5:12

> For, lo, the winter is past, the rain is over and gone;
> The flowers appear on the earth; the time of the singing of birds is come, and the voice of the turtle is heard in our land.
>
> SONG OF SOLOMON 2:11–12

Disillusionment
and Disappointment

"The best-laid schemes o' mice and men / Gang aft a-gley," wrote Scottish poet Robert Burns, meaning that very often our plans for the future can be as easily upset as those of a tiny, helpless mouse.

When things do not go as we had hoped, we often are disappointed. If other people have had their share in causing this disappointment, we are still further disillusioned. How can a good friend treat us thusly? Why are not certain family members more understanding? Is there any reason why we weren't promoted to a better job? There are many reasons for us to experience disillusionment and disappointment, but it is important to be able to take the long view, to see things in their proper perspective.

The disappointments of this world are only temporary, and we must think of them as such, and strengthen ourselves to cope with them. Spiritual strength can aid us in dealing with material disappointments, and to gain more of that strength, we might remember Paul's words:

> For our light affliction, which is but for a moment, worketh for us a far more exceeding and eternal weight of glory;
> While we look not at the things which are seen, but at the things which are not seen: for the things which are seen are temporal; but the things which are not seen are eternal.
>
> II CORINTHIANS 4:17–18

Though others may disappoint us, we must remember that there is One to whom we can always turn:

Out of the depths have I cried unto thee, O Lord.

Lord, hear my voice: let thine ears be attentive to the voice of my supplications.

If thou, Lord, shouldest mark iniquities, O Lord, who shall stand?

But there is forgiveness with thee, that thou mayest be feared.

I wait for the Lord, my soul doth wait, and in his word do I hope.

My soul waiteth for the Lord more than they that watch for the morning: I say, more than they that watch for the morning.

PSALMS 130:1–6

We must recognize that some of the disappointments and disillusionments we experience may be the Lord's way of testing us, or preparing us for what lies ahead.

And ye have forgotten the exhortation which speaketh unto you as unto children, My son, despise not thou the chastening of the Lord, nor faint when thou art rebuked of him:

For whom the Lord loveth he chasteneth, and scourgeth every son whom he receiveth.

If ye endure chastening, God dealeth with you as with sons; for what son is he whom the father chasteneth not?

HEBREWS 12:5–7

Now no chastening for the present seemeth to be joyous, but grievous: nevertheless, afterward it yieldeth the peaceable fruit of righteousness unto them which are exercised thereby.

HEBREWS 12:11

Very often, our disappointments with this life are based on the feeling that we are being singled out unjustly.

Why do others have so much more than we have? Why are our neighbors, our friends, more fortunate than we are? Soon, if we continue thinking in this vein, our disillusionment turns to bitterness, and then we are even less able to cope with our problems. But we must remember that all things come to all people. And our disappointment of today may be shared by someone else tomorrow. In fact, when we are happy, why do we not then wonder why others are not as happy as we?

> I returned, and saw under the sun, that the race is not to the swift, nor the battle to the strong, neither yet bread to the wise, nor yet riches to men of understanding, nor yet favor to men of skill; but time and chance happeneth to them all.
>
> For man also knoweth not his time: as the fishes that are taken in an evil net, and as the birds that are caught in the snare; so are the sons of men snared in an evil time, when it falleth suddenly upon them.
>
> This wisdom have I seen also under the sun, and it seemed great unto me:
>
> There was a little city, and few men within it; and there came a great king against it, and besieged it, and built great bulwarks against it.
>
> Now there was found in it a poor wise man, and he by his wisdom delivered the city; yet no man remembered that same poor man.
>
> Then said I, Wisdom is better than strength: nevertheless the poor man's wisdom is despised, and his words are not heard.
>
> ECCLESIASTES 9:11–16

If you know that you have done a fine and good deed, do not be disappointed if others do not recognize your goodness, for you can be sure that your good deed has not gone unrecognized:

> The Lord will not suffer the soul of the righteous to famish: but he casteth away the substance of the wicked.
>
> PROVERBS 10:3

> Blessings are upon the head of the just: but violence covereth the mouth of the wicked.

The memory of the just is blessed: but the name of the wicked shall rot.

The wise in heart will receive commandments: but a prating fool shall fall.

He that walketh uprightly walketh surely: but he that perverteth his ways shall be known.

PROVERBS 10:6–9

Remember, at all times, that your disappointments lie with men—never with God or with Jesus. Understanding this, you know that you are never alone, and ask for divine comfort:

Thy righteousness also, O God, is very high, who hast done great things: O God, who is like unto thee!

Thou, which hast showed me great and sore troubles, shall quicken me again, and shalt bring me up again from the depths of the earth.

Thou shalt increase my greatness, and comfort me on every side.

PSALMS 71:19–21

How much disillusionment may we allow ourselves, when we remember that our Saviour knew he would be betrayed, yet continued to serve mankind so lovingly:

And while they abode in Galilee, Jesus said unto them, The Son of man shall be betrayed into the hands of men:

And they shall kill him, and the third day he shall be raised again. And they were exceeding sorry.

MATTHEW 17:22–23

And it came to pass, when Jesus had finished all these sayings, he said unto his disciples,

Ye know that after two days is the feast of the passover, and the Son of man is betrayed to be crucified.

Then assembled together the chief priests, and the scribes, and the elders of the people, unto the palace of the high priest, who was called Caiaphas,

And consulted that they might take Jesus by subtilty, and kill him.

MATTHEW 26:1–4

If Jesus could accept Peter's denial of Him, surely we should be able to face everything that comes our way:

Jesus said unto him, Verily I say unto thee, That this night, before the cock crow, thou shalt deny me thrice.

Peter said unto him, Though I should die with thee, yet will not I deny thee. Likewise said all the disciples.

MATTHEW 26:34–36

Now Peter sat without in the palace: and a damsel came unto him, saying, Thou also wast with Jesus of Galilee.

But he denied before them all, saying, I know not what thou sayest.

And when he was gone out into the porch, another maid saw him, and said unto them that were there, This fellow was also with Jesus of Nazareth.

And again he denied with an oath, I do not know the man.

And after a while came unto him they that stood by, and said to Peter, Surely thou art also one of them; for thy speech betrayeth thee.

Then began he to curse and to swear, saying, I know not the man. And immediately the cock crew.

And Peter remembered the word of Jesus, which said unto him, Before the cock crow, thou shalt deny me thrice. And he went out, and wept bitterly.

MATTHEW 26:69–75

When facing disappointments, remember that you are not the first—nor the last—to do so. But even as Daniel was comforted, so shall you be comforted, too:

Then there came again and touched me one like the appearance of a man, and he strengthened me,

And said, O man greatly beloved, fear not: peace be unto thee, be strong, yea, be strong. And when he had spoken unto me, I was strengthened, and said, Let my Lord speak; for thou hast strengthened me.

DANIEL 10:18–19

And many of them that sleep in the dust of the earth shall awake, some to everlasting life, and some to shame and everlasting contempt.

And they that be wise shall shine as the brightness of the firmament; and they that turn many to righteousness as the stars for ever and ever.

DANIEL 12:2–3

Envy

Blessed is the person who can say along with William Shakespeare: "I am a true laborer: I earn that I eat, get that I wear, owe no man hate, envy no man's happiness, glad of other men's good."

Too often, however, we do envy others' happiness, or their material possessions. Instead of counting our own blessings, we spend much time jealously counting the blessings of others.

This smallness of spirit, this unkindness of heart, is unworthy of the sacrifice made for us by our Saviour. Whom does envy truly harm? It harms the envious, taking from them the generosity of spirit which might make them truly happy.

If envy possesses you from time to time, recollect:

> Thou shalt not covet thy neighbor's house, thou shalt not covet thy neighbor's wife, nor his manservant, nor his maidservant, nor his ox, nor his ass, nor any thing that is thy neighbor's.
>
> EXODUS 20:17

Do you find yourself—despite your own best intentions —envying the wealth of others? If these feelings are part of you, try to remember:

> Better is little with the fear of the Lord than great treasure and trouble therewith.
> Better is a dinner of herbs where love is, than a stalled ox and hatred therewith.
>
> PROVERBS 15:16–17

How much better is it to get wisdom than gold! And to get understanding rather to be chosen than silver!

PROVERBS 16:16

Perhaps your moments of envy are concerned with people whom you know to be less than good or righteous, but who seem to succeed despite their devious ways or their unkindness. Think again when you are feeling this way, and ask yourself how can you possibly envy a bad person?

And while it is not for you to judge another, judgment will come.

Fret not thyself because of evildoers, neither be thou envious against the workers of iniquity.

For they shall soon be cut down like the grass, and wither as the green herb.

Trust in the Lord, and do good; so shalt thou dwell in the land, and verily thou shalt be fed.

Delight thyself also in the Lord; and he shall give thee the desires of thine heart.

Commit thy way unto the Lord; trust also in him; and he shall bring it to pass.

And he shall bring forth thy righteousness as the light, and thy judgment as the noonday.

Rest in the Lord, and wait patiently for him: fret not thyself because of him who prospereth in his way, because of the man who bringeth wicked devices to pass.

Cease from anger, and forsake wrath: fret not thyself in any wise to do evil.

For evildoers shall be cut off: but those that wait upon the Lord, they shall inherit the earth.

PSALMS 37:1-9

Wait on the Lord, and keep his way, and he shall exalt thee to inherit the land: when the wicked are cut off, thou shalt see it.

I have seen the wicked in great power, and spreading himself like a green bay tree.

Yet he passed away, and, lo, he was not: yea, I sought him, but he could not be found.

PSALMS 37:34-36

When envying the material treasures of others, remember that it is the treasure of the soul and of the spirit that is truly important. It is because of this that Jesus warned His disciples about the dangers of covetousness:

> And one of the company said unto him, Master, speak to my brother, that he divide the inheritance with me.
>
> And he said unto him, Man, who made me a judge or a divider over you?
>
> And he said unto them, Take heed, and beware of covetousness: for a man's life consisteth not in the abundance of the things which he possesseth.
>
> And he spake a parable unto them, saying, The ground of a certain rich man brought forth plentifully:
>
> And he thought within himself, saying, What shall I do, because I have no room where to bestow my fruits?
>
> And he said, This will I do: I will pull down my barns, and build greater; and there will I bestow all my fruits and my goods.
>
> And I will say to my soul, Soul thou hast much goods laid up for many years; take thine ease, eat, drink, and be merry.
>
> But God said unto him, Thou fool, this night thy soul shall be required of thee: then whose shall those things be, which thou hast provided?
>
> So is he that layeth up treasure for himself, and is not rich toward God.
>
> LUKE 12:13–21

Perhaps the envy you feel is for the talents of other people; remember, though, that there is more than one kind of talent, all come from God, and we are all blessed by different abilities.

> Now there are diversities of gifts, but the same Spirit.
>
> And there are differences of administrations, but the same Lord.
>
> And there are diversities of operations, but it is the same God which worketh all in all.

But the manifestation of the Spirit is given to every man to profit withal.

For to one is given by the Spirit the word of wisdom; to another the word of knowledge by the same Spirit;

To another faith by the same Spirit; to another the gifts of healing by the same Spirit;

To another the working of miracles; to another prophecy; to another discerning of spirits; to another divers kinds of tongues; to another the interpretation of tongues;

But all these worketh that one and the selfsame Spirit, dividing to every man severally as he will.

I CORINTHIANS 12:4–11

Remember, then, that whatever your role in life, if you do things with goodwill, and with a hopeful spirit, whatever has been given to you to do is important.

There is no need to feel envious of anyone else: all souls are equal in importance.

And God hath set some in the church, first apostles, secondarily prophets, thirdly teachers, after that miracles, then gifts of healings, helps, governments, diversities of tongues.

Are all apostles? Are all prophets? Are all teachers? Are all workers of miracles?

Have all the gifts of healing? Do all speak with tongues? Do all interpret?

But covet earnestly the best gifts: and yet show I unto you a more excellent way.

I CORINTHIANS 12:28–31

There is an important difference between being truly wise, and merely appearing to be wise. The truly wise person is never envious:

Who is a wise man and endued with knowledge among you? Let him show out of a good conversation his works with meekness of wisdom.

But if ye have bitter envying and strife in your hearts, glory not, and lie not against the truth.

This wisdom descendeth not from above, but is earthly, sensual, devilish.

For where envying and strife is, there is confusion and every evil work.

But the wisdom that is from above is first pure, then peaceable, gentle, and easy to be entreated, full of mercy and good fruits, without partiality, and without hypocrisy.

And the fruit of righteousness is sown in peace of them that make peace.

JAMES 3:13–18

If we live in the Spirit, let us also walk in the Spirit.

Let us not be desirous of vain glory, provoking one another, envying one another.

GALATIANS 5:25–26

Failure

You have failed—perhaps not once, but many times. Your failure lies heavily upon your soul. You brood about it, think about it, wonder why you are not adequate to the tasks you have set yourself.

Perhaps it is time to examine the areas of your failure more closely. If you have done your best, worked honestly, tried your utmost, can you really believe that you have failed?

Take comfort in the knowledge that there are other ways to observe your actions; the surface appearance is not all that matters; motive and intent are also important.

> But the Lord said unto Samuel, Look not on his countenance, or on the height of his stature; because I have refused him: for the Lord seeth not as man seeth; for man looketh on the outward appearance, but the Lord looketh on the heart.
>
> I SAMUEL 16:7

As you move forward to accomplish the next task of your life, don't dwell on past failures, but continue your work with hope, understanding that you are being observed first of all, by God, and only afterward by your fellowmen:

> And whatsoever ye do, do it heartily, as to the Lord, and not unto men.
>
> COLOSSIANS 3:23

Remember that your sense of failure today can be changed to one of peace and calm tomorrow. Our Saviour has enough love for all. Isaac blessed his son, Jacob. But when his son, Esau, pleaded for a blessing, Isaac blessed him as well. If Isaac could bless his two children, we must understand that God can bless us all, relieving us of our feelings of failure and inadequacy.

> And Esau said unto his father, Hast thou but one blessing, my father? Bless me, even me also, O my father. And Esau lifted up his voice, and wept.
>
> And Isaac his father answered and said unto him, Behold, thy dwelling shall be the fatness of the earth, and of the dew of heaven from above;
>
> And by thy sword shalt thou live, and shalt serve thy brother; and it shall come to pass when thou shalt have the dominion, that thou shalt break his yoke from off thy neck.
>
> GENESIS 27:38–40

And when Joseph was falsely accused, and put into prison, the Lord was with him, and allowed no harm to come to him:

> But the Lord was with Joseph, and showed him mercy, and gave him favor in the sight of the keeper of the prison.
>
> And the keeper of the prison committed to Joseph's hand all the prisoners that were in the prison; and whatsoever they did there, he was the doer of it.
>
> The keeper of the prison looked not to any thing that was under his hand; because the Lord was with him, and that which he did, the Lord made it to prosper.
>
> GENESIS 39:21–23

Often, after an experience of failure, one is beset by the fear of failing again, but go forth with confidence—not in the power of your own efforts, but in the power of the Lord:

> Blessed is the man that trusteth in the Lord, and whose hope the Lord is.

For he shall be as a tree planteth by the waters, and
that spreadeth out her roots by the river, and shall not
see when heat cometh, but her leaf shall be green; and
shall not be careful in the year of drought, neither shall
cease from yielding fruit.

JEREMIAH 17:7–8

The Lord God is my strength, and he will make my
feet like hinds' feet, and he will make me to walk upon
mine high places. To the chief singer on my stringed
instruments.

HABAKKUK 3:19

Be merciful unto me, O God, be merciful unto me:
for my soul trusteth in thee: yea, in the shadow of thy
wings will I make my refuge, until these calamities be
overpast.

I will cry unto God most high; unto God that per-
formeth all things for me.

He shall send from heaven, and save me from the reproach of him that would swallow me up. Selah. God
shall send forth his mercy and his truth.

PSALMS 57:1–3

Failures in material things are certainly not as important as failure of the spirit. But these failings can be
fought against and overcome by standing fast in the light
of belief:

Now we beseech you, brethren, by the coming of our
Lord Jesus Christ, and by our gathering together unto
him,

That ye be not soon shaken in mind, or be troubled,
neither by spirit, nor by word, nor by letter as from us,
as that the day of Christ is at hand.

II THESSALONIANS 2:1–2

Faithlessness

Is there anything sadder than the person who is faithless? This person does not know the meaning of commitment —whether it is to God, or to others, or even to himself.

Possibly, from time to time, you, too, have found yourself faithless toward a friend or a loved one, or lacking in faith toward God and our Saviour.

Faithlessness of any sort is doubly harmful: it hurts the person who is faithless, and it saddens and pains the one toward whom the faithlessness is directed.

"Our hearts, our hopes, are all with thee," wrote the poet Henry Wadsworth Longfellow, "Our hearts, our hopes, our prayers, our tears, / our faith triumphant O'er our fears, / Are all with thee—are all with thee!"

With help from above, we, too, can learn to keep the faith with God and our Saviour, with the people whom we care for.

> And when they were come to the multitude, there came to him a certain man, kneeling down to him, and saying,
>
> Lord, have mercy on my son: for he is lunatic, and sore vexed: for ofttimes he falleth into the fire, and oft into the water.
>
> And I brought him to thy disciples, and they could not cure him.
>
> Then Jesus answered and said, O faithless and perverse generation, how long shall I be with you? How long shall I suffer you? Bring him hither to me.

And Jesus rebuked the devil; and he departed out of him: and the child was cured from that very hour.

Then came the disciples to Jesus apart, and said, Why could not we cast him out?

And Jesus said unto them, Because of your unbelief: for verily I say unto you, If ye have faith as a grain of mustard seed, ye shall say unto this mountain, Remove hence to yonder place; and it shall remove; and nothing shall be impossible unto you.

MATTHEW 17:14–20

Faith—true faith—is the source of many miracles; faith makes all things possible for those who truly believe:

By faith he forsook Egypt, not fearing the wrath of the king: for he endured, as seeing him who is invisible.

HEBREWS 11:27

By faith they passed through the Red sea as by dry land: which the Egyptians assaying to do were drowned.

By faith the walls of Jericho fell down, after they were compassed about seven days.

HEBREWS 11:29–30

Understand that, if you have faith, it so often is not enough to say so, you must also behave as one of the faithful:

What doth it profit, my brethren, though a man say he hath faith, and have not works? Can faith save him?

If a brother or sister be naked, and destitute of daily food,

And one of you say unto them, Depart in peace, be ye warmed and filled; notwithstanding ye give them not those things which are needful to the body; what doth it profit?

Even so faith, if it hath not works, is dead, being alone.

JAMES 2:14–17

> Was not Abraham our father justified by works, when he had offered Isaac his son upon the altar?
>
> Seest thou how faith wrought with his works, and by works was faith made perfect?
>
> JAMES 2:21–22

How do you acquire faith? How can you learn to be faithful in thought, in feeling, and in deeds? If you find faithfulness difficult to acquire, don't be afraid to ask for help:

> Ask, and it shall be given you; seek, and ye shall find; knock, and it shall be opened unto you:
>
> For every one that asketh receiveth; and he that seeketh findeth; and to him that knocketh it shall be opened.
>
> MATTHEW 7:7–8

Remember the wondrous occurrences that were vouchsafed to those who had faith:

> And what shall I more say? For the time would fail me to tell of Gideon, and of Barak, and of Samson, and of Jephthah; of David also, and Samuel, and of the prophets:
>
> Who through faith subdued kingdoms, wrought righteousness, obtained promises, stopped the mouths of lions,
>
> Quenched the violence of fire, escaped the edge of the sword, out of weakness were made strong, waxed valiant in fight, turned to flight the armies of the aliens.
>
> HEBRFWS 11:32–34

Just as you must try always to be faithful to God, His commandments, and to His beloved Son, Jesus Christ, so should you also be faithful to the people whom you love. Remember the words of King Solomon:

> For the lips of a strange woman drop as a honeycomb, and her mouth is smoother than oil:

But her end is bitter as wormwood, sharp as a two-edged sword.

Her feet go down to death; her steps take hold on hell.

PROVERBS 5:3–5

Drink waters out of thine own cistern, and running waters out of thine own well.

Let thy fountains be dispersed abroad, and rivers of waters in the streets.

Let them be only thine own, and not strangers' with thee.

Let thy fountain be blessed: and rejoice with the wife of thy youth.

Let her be as the loving hind and pleasant roe; let her breasts satisfy thee at all times; and be thou ravished always with her love.

PROVERBS 5:15–19

Can a man take fire in his bosom, and his clothes not be burned?

Can one go upon hot coals, and his feet not be burned?

So he that goeth in to his neighbor's wife; whosoever toucheth her shall not be innocent.

PROVERBS 6:27–29

As King Solomon spoke of the importance of faithfulness in husbands, so King Lemuel spoke of the importance of faithfulness in wives:

Who can find a virtuous woman? For her price is far above rubies.

The heart of her husband doth safely trust in her, so that he shall have no need of spoil.

She will do him good and not evil all the days of her life.

PROVERBS 31:10–12

To strengthen your faith, read the Holy Scriptures, and pay close attention to the words, understanding that it is faith which leads to true righteousness:

For Christ is the end of the law for righteousness to every one that believeth.

For Moses describeth the righteousness which is of the law, That the man which doeth these things shall live by them.

But the righteousness which is of faith speaketh on this wise, Say not in thine heart, Who shall ascend into heaven? (that is, to bring Christ down from above:)

Or, Who shall descend into the deep? (that is, to bring up Christ again from the dead.)

But what saith it? The word is nigh thee, even in thy mouth, and in thy heart: that is, the word of faith, which we preach;

That if thou shalt confess with thy mouth the Lord Jesus, and shalt believe in thine heart that God hath raised him from the dead, thou shalt be saved.

ROMANS 10:4–9

The most faithful of us at times are so tried that we may feel our faith wavering. When that happens to you, think positively; remember how Jesus fed the five thousand:

When Jesus then lifted up his eyes, and saw a great company come unto him, he saith unto Philip, Whence shall we buy bread, that these may eat?

And this he said to prove him: for he himself knew what he would do.

Philip answered him, Two hundred pennyworth of bread is not sufficient for them, that every one of them may take a little.

One of his disciples, Andrew, Simon Peter's brother, saith unto him,

There is a lad here, which hath five barley loaves, and two small fishes: but what are they among so many?

And Jesus said, Make the men sit down. Now there was much grass in the place. So the men sat down, in number about five thousand.

And Jesus took the loaves; and when he had given

thanks, he distributed to the disciples, and the disciples to them that were set down; and likewise of the fishes as much as they would.

When they were filled, he said unto his disciples, Gather up the fragments that remain, that nothing be lost.

Therefore they gathered them together, and filled twelve baskets with the fragments of the five barley loaves, which remained over and above unto them that had eaten.

Then those men, when they had seen the miracle that Jesus did, said, This is of a truth that prophet that should come into the world.

JOHN 6:5–14

Continue refreshing your faith, and remember Jesus at Capernaum:

And when even was now come, his disciples went down unto the sea,

And entered into a ship, and went over the sea toward Capernaum. And it was now dark, and Jesus was not come to them.

And the sea arose by reason of a great wind that blew.

So when they had rowed about five and twenty or thirty furlongs, they see Jesus walking on the sea, and drawing nigh unto the ship: and they were afraid.

But he saith unto them, It is I; be not afraid.

Then they willingly received him into the ship: and immediately the ship was at the land whither they went.

JOHN 6:16–21

His disciples' ship followed the true path, once Jesus was aboard, and your faith can help you find the true path as well. Ask for faith, even as the apostles asked:

And the apostles said unto the Lord, Increase our faith.

And the Lord said, If ye had faith as a grain of mustard seed, ye might say unto this sycamine tree, Be thou plucked up by the root, and be thou planted in the sea; and it should obey you.

LUKE 17:5–6

Faithfulness can fill you with tranquillity, as you remember His words:

Peace I leave with you, my peace I give unto you: not as the world giveth, give I unto you. Let not your heart be troubled, neither let it be afraid.

JOHN 14:27

He that is faithful in that which is least is faithful also in much: and he that is unjust in the least is unjust also in much.

If therefore ye have not been faithful in the unrighteous mammon, who will commit to your trust the true riches?

And if ye have not been faithful in that which is another man's, who shall give you that which is your own?

LUKE 16:10–12

Fear and Anxiety

Fear and anxiety are supposedly ills of modern times. But didn't the ancient Israelites experience the same feelings in Egypt? Wasn't Daniel fearful in the fiery furnace? And weren't the disciples most anxious and fearful when Jesus was led before Pilate?

Fear and anxiety have been part of life ever since Adam and Eve were driven from the Garden of Eden. Sometimes, though, our fears and our anxieties reach such mammoth proportions that we cannot cope with our feelings. Indeed, our fears may become so intense and so consuming that they do not allow us to solve our problems.

When that happens, we must turn to the Bible for help and for guidance, and within the pages of this Good Book we will find:

> The Lord is my light and my salvation; whom shall I fear? The Lord is the strength of my life; of whom shall I be afraid?
>
> PSALMS 27:1

> Though a host should encamp against me, my heart shall not fear: though war should rise against me, in this will I be confident.
>
> PSALMS 27:3

Are our fears real, or are they imaginary? Are we anxious for ourselves, or for our loved ones? Is it the future that worries us, or the present? Whatever the basis of our fears, we will be able to cope with our inner turmoil if we believe wholly in the love of God:

> For God hath not given us the spirit of fear; but of power, and of love, and of a sound mind.
>
> II TIMOTHY 1:7

> Have not I commanded thee? Be strong and of a good courage; be not afraid, neither be thou dismayed: for the Lord thy God is with thee whithersoever thou goest.
>
> JOSHUA 1:9

When you fear the most is the time to pray for help and for guidance.

Jonah was most fearful when he was in the belly of the whale, yet even there he prayed:

> Then Jonah prayed unto the Lord his God out of the fish's belly,
> And said, I cried by reason of mine affliction unto the Lord, and he heard me; out of the belly of hell cried I, and thou heardest my voice.
>
> JONAH 2:1–2

Even people of great faith are frequently fearful of death, and anxious about illness; but these fears and anxieties pass quickly when we remember:

> And, behold, a certain lawyer stood up, and tempted him, saying, Master, what shall I do to inherit eternal life?
> He said unto him, What is written in the law? How readest thou?
> And he answering said, Thou shalt love the Lord thy God with all thy heart, and with all thy soul, and with all thy strength, and with all thy mind; and thy neighbor as thyself.

And he said unto him, Thou hast answered right; this do, and thou shalt live.

LUKE 10:25–28

Behold, God is my salvation; I will trust, and not be afraid: for the Lord Jehovah is my strength and my song; he also is become my salvation.

ISAIAH 12:2

How can we fear for our lives here on earth, when we know that what is important is our souls?

And fear not them which kill the body, but are not able to kill the soul: but rather fear him which is able to destroy both soul and body in hell.

MATTHEW 10:28

The Psalms teach us that during the worst of times we are never alone if we have faith:

God is our refuge and strength, a very present help in trouble.
Therefore will not we fear, though the earth be removed, and though the mountains be carried into the midst of the sea;
Though the waters thereof roar and be troubled, though the mountains shake with the swelling thereof. Selah.

PSALMS 46:1–3

What time I am afraid, I will trust in thee.
In God I will praise his word, in God I have put my trust; I will not fear what flesh can do unto me.

PSALMS 56:3–4

Love of God and of Jesus, and of those around us, is the best antidote to fear. Secure in this love, our fear disappears:

For this is the message that ye heard from the beginning, that we should love one another.

I JOHN 3:11

We know that we have passed from death unto life, because we love the brethren. He that loveth not his brother abideth in death.

I JOHN 3:14

Whosoever shall confess that Jesus is the Son of God, God dwelleth in him, and he in God.

And we have known and believed the love that God hath to us. God is love; and he that dwelleth in love dwelleth in God, and God in him.

Herein is our love made perfect, that we have boldness in the day of judgment: because as he is, so are we in this world.

There is no fear in love; but perfect love casteth out fear: because fear hath torment. He that feareth is not made perfect in love.

We love him, because he first loved us.

I JOHN 4:15–19

Fear thou not; for I am with thee: be not dismayed; for I am thy God: I will strengthen thee; yea, I will help thee; yea, I will uphold thee with the right hand of my righteousness.

ISAIAH 41:10

Fear and anxiety are the enemies of joy; they rob us of our peace of mind. If we put our trust in the Lord, our peace of mind will be restored, and with it, our joy.

Let us remember that we are in God's hands. We can rest quietly, because we have been given much assurance:

For I the Lord thy God will hold thy right hand, saying unto thee, Fear not; I will help thee.

ISAIAH 41:13

Fear them not therefore: for there is nothing covered, that shall not be revealed; and hid, that shall not be known.

MATTHEW 10:26

I am the door: by me if any man enter in, he shall be saved, and shall go in and out, and find pasture.

JOHN 10:9

I am the good shepherd: the good shepherd giveth his life for the sheep.

JOHN 10:11

Our fears, our anxieties, they lessen, and may even disappear completely when we remember:

And this is the record, that God hath given to us eternal life, and this life is in his Son.

He that hath the Son hath life; and he that hath not the Son of God hath not life.

These things have I written unto you that believe on the name of the Son of God; that ye may know that ye have eternal life, and that ye may believe on the name of the Son of God.

I JOHN 5:11–13

Ye are all the children of light, and the children of the day: we are not of the night, nor of darkness.

I THESSALONIANS 5:5

Wherefore comfort yourselves together, and edify one another, even as also ye do.

I THESSALONIANS 5:11

Rejoice evermore.
Pray without ceasing.
In every thing give thanks: for this is the will of God in Christ Jesus concerning you.

I THESSALONIANS 5:16–18

Frustration

Oh, those days when you feel so frustrated! All your fine plans seem to fail; you're baffled at every turn. You are doing your very best, trying your hardest, but yet, nothing seems to turn out right for you. You feel so disappointed and thwarted, that you're just about ready to give up.

Perhaps one of your problems is that you have been trying to do everything by yourself. It is wonderful to make a great effort, but why not avail yourself of the spiritual aid that is waiting for you in the pages of the Bible?

When things seem to be going especially wrong, consult the following passages that advise patience. This advice is centuries old, and has been helping all those who would be helped. You cannot accomplish all you would do in one day. As Paul advised,

> Wherefore seeing we also are compassed about with so great a cloud of witnesses, let us lay aside every weight, and the sin which doth so easily beset us, and let us run with patience the race that is set before us.
>
> HEBREWS 12:1

Perhaps things seem impossible in the beginning, but take heart, it is the end result that is important:

> Better is the end of a thing than the beginning thereof: and the patient in spirit is better than the proud in spirit.
>
> ECCLESIASTES 7:8

When deep frustration assails you, remember that the truly wonderful and miraculous things of this world must be awaited with patience:

> Be patient therefore, brethren, unto the coming of the Lord. Behold, the husbandman waiteth for the precious fruit of the earth, and hath long patience for it, until he receive the early and latter rain.
>
> Be ye also patient; stablish your hearts: for the coming of the Lord draweth nigh.
>
> JAMES 5:7–8

Your problem may be that you yearn too much for worldly things, and that you do not give enough thought to the problems of your soul. Your frustration may be rooted in your own inability to understand that life was never meant to be a constant ascent, but that we all experience valleys and sloughs.

The Scriptures tell us very clearly that there is a special time allotted for all things in this world:

> To every thing there is a season, and a time to every purpose under the heaven:
>
> A time to be born, and a time to die; a time to plant, and a time to pluck up that which is planted;
>
> A time to kill, and a time to heal; a time to break down, and a time to build up;
>
> A time to weep, and a time to laugh; a time to mourn, and a time to dance;
>
> A time to cast away stones, and a time to gather stones together; a time to embrace, and a time to refrain from embracing;
>
> A time to get, and a time to lose; a time to keep, and a time to cast away;
>
> A time to rend, and a time to sew; a time to keep silence, and a time to speak;
>
> A time to love, and a time to hate; a time of war, and a time of peace.
>
> ECCLESIASTES 3:1–8

Sometimes your frustration drives you to unreasoning anger, and you do things you know are wrong. Now you are doubly frustrated: you have accomplished nothing useful, and you have not behaved according to the precepts of our Great Teacher, Jesus.

Don't give up on yourself! The Saviour hasn't. He who forgave Peter can forgive you if you're truly penitent:

> And he said, I tell thee, Peter, the cock shall not crow this day, before that thou shalt thrice deny that thou knowest me.
>
> LUKE 22:34

> And when they had kindled a fire in the midst of the hall, and were set down together, Peter sat down among them.
>
> But a certain maid beheld him as he sat by the fire, and earnestly looked upon him, and said, This man was also with him.
>
> And he denied him, saying, Woman, I know him not.
>
> And after a little while another saw him, and said, Thou art also of them. And Peter said, Man, I am not.
>
> And about the space of one hour after another confidently affirmed, saying, Of a truth this fellow also was with him: for he is a Galilean.
>
> And Peter said, Man, I know not what thou sayest. And immediately, while he yet spake, the cock crew.
>
> And the Lord turned, and looked upon Peter. And Peter remembered the word of the Lord, how he had said unto him, Before the cock crow, thou shalt deny me thrice.
>
> And Peter went out, and wept bitterly.
>
> LUKE 22:55–62

> For Christ also hath once suffered for sins, the just for the unjust, that he might bring us to God, being put to death in the flesh, but quickened by the Spirit.
>
> I PETER 3:18

If it is your own deeds and lack of spiritual values that frustrate you the most, remember the parable of the lost sheep:

> How think ye? If a man have a hundred sheep, and one of them be gone astray, doth he not leave the ninety and nine, and goeth into the mountains, and seeketh that which is gone astray?
>
> And if so be that he find it, verily I say unto you, he rejoiceth more of that sheep, than of the ninety and nine which went not astray.
>
> MATTHEW 18:12–13

All your frustrations will lessen, once you accept completely that salvation can be yours, through our Lord, Jesus Christ. You will know peace, and you will be able to say:

> Finally, brethren, whatsoever things are true, whatsoever things are honest, whatsoever things are just, whatsoever things are pure, whatsoever things are lovely, whatsoever things are of good report; if there be any virtue, and if there be any praise, think on these things.
>
> Those things, which ye have both learned, and received, and heard, and seen in me, do: and the God of peace shall be with you.
>
> But I rejoiced in the Lord greatly, that now at the last your care of me hath flourished again; wherein ye were also careful, but ye lacked opportunity.
>
> Not that I speak in respect of want: for I have learned, in whatsoever state I am, therewith to be content.
>
> I know both how to be abased, and I know how to abound: every where and in all things I am instructed both to be full and to be hungry, both to abound and to suffer need.
>
> PHILIPPIANS 4:8–12

To avoid a sense of frustration based on imaginary ills and slights, one must be supremely honest with oneself.

Are you frustrated because others have more wealth, more possessions, than you have? This is not frustration. Call it by its real name: covetousness. Instead of envying others for what they may own, do your best to build up spiritual riches:

> Let your conversation be without covetousness; and be content with such things as ye have: for he hath said, I will never leave thee, nor forsake thee.
>
> HEBREWS 13:5

All of us feel frustrated when we realize how little we know, and how many faults we have. It is important to understand that only God has perfect knowledge, it was given to us to strive toward knowledge, just as we strive toward salvation. Turn to God with prayers, beseeching Him to show you the path toward greater wisdom:

> But let patience have her perfect work, that ye may be perfect and entire, wanting nothing.
>
> If any of you lack wisdom, let him ask of God, that giveth to all men liberally, and upbraideth not; and it shall be given him.
>
> But let him ask in faith, nothing wavering: for he that wavereth is like a wave of the sea driven with the wind and tossed.
>
> JAMES 1:4-6

Cultivating a humble attitude can also do much to lessen frustration. Do you think you are so perfect that it is impossible for you to make a mistake? If this is the way you feel about yourself, you will, of course, feel frustrated. Accept the fact that you are, as are all of us, imperfect. This will help you when it's time to face both the triumphs and setbacks that are part of life:

> For what glory is it, if, when ye be buffeted for your faults, ye shall take it patiently? but if, when ye do well,

and suffer for it, ye take it patiently, this is acceptable
with God.

I PETER 2:20

Do not let the actions of others add to your frustrations.
Perhaps you have said to yourself: I have done good
things, yet others don't recognize them. Remember that
the good done by our Lord, Jesus Christ, was also not
recognized by many:

> For even hereunto were ye called: because Christ also
> suffered for us, leaving us an example, that ye should
> follow his steps:
> Who did no sin, neither was guile found in his mouth:
> Who, when he was reviled, reviled not again; when he
> suffered, he threatened not; but committed himself to
> him that judgeth righteously.

I PETER 2:21–23

Understand that you are not the ultimate judge of your
own deeds. Your frustrated feelings will lessen when you
work toward goals that you hope will be pleasing to God
and His Son:

> Let the words of my mouth, and the meditation of my
> heart, be acceptable in thy sight, O Lord, my strength,
> and my redeemer.

PSALMS 19:14

Try to be fair toward others, as you would have them
be fair toward you. If you are not unreasonable in your
expectations about other people, you will not feel so
baffled or frustrated by their actions, or behavior, toward
you:

> For whatsoever things were written aforetime were
> written for our learning, that we through patience and
> comfort of the scriptures might have hope.

Now the God of patience and consolation grant you to be like-minded one toward another according to Christ Jesus.

ROMANS 15:4–5

If you're having an especially bad day, if your nights are filled with wakefulness, if you're sure that nothing can go right for you and that your life will be filled with frustrations forever, remember the promise given to us by blessed Jesus, and you will realize that there is an order to all our lives, even though the order may not be apparent to you. Once you can fully believe in the orderliness of God's world, you will understand that He can make all things possible:

Jesus said unto him, If thou canst believe, all things are possible to him that believeth.

MARK 9:23

Greed

Greed is a most unattractive characteristic. And yet, it is a trait that the best person may evince at one time or another. It is easy to condemn another for greed, but haven't we all been guilty of greediness at different times in our lives?

Greed can take on various manifestations; it can hide behind many a mask, wear many different guises and costumes. We may experience greed for food—a need not based on actual hunger, but rather on an unexplainable desire to acquire more sustenance than our bodies actually require.

Greed can indicate its unwanted presence in far more complicated ways: there is the greed for things, for objects that are not at all necessary to true happiness; then there is the greed for money, for more money than we actually need; there may also be the greed for power, the greed for fame or recognition, the greed to be loved more than others are loved.

The greedy person is an unpleasant person, not easily liked, not generally respected; but the person who suffers from greed, and who recognizes that he *is* suffering, can be helped when he understands that all the things, all the possessions of this world, are not true treasures but actually hindrances that hold us back from acquiring peace of spirit:

> Lay not up for yourselves treasures upon earth, where moth and rust doth corrupt, and where thieves break through and steal:

But lay up for yourselves treasures in heaven, where neither moth nor rust doth corrupt, and where thieves do not break through nor steal:

For where your treasure is, there will your heart be also.

MATTHEW 6:19–21

The Son of God has never asked us to be content with nothing at all. In addition to the spiritual gifts He has given to us in bountiful supply, He has also understood that we need a degree of comfort while we are on His Father's earth. However, in His name, we must learn to recognize the difference between having enough and pining for excess:

And having food and raiment, let us be therewith content.

But they that will be rich fall into temptation and a snare, and into many foolish and hurtful lusts, which drown men in destruction and perdition.

For the love of money is the root of all evil: which while some coveted after, they have erred from the faith, and pierced themselves through with many sorrows.

But thou, O man of God, flee these things; and follow after righteousness, godliness, faith, love, patience, meekness.

Fight the good fight of faith, lay hold on eternal life, whereunto thou art also called, and hast professed a good profession before many witnesses.

I TIMOTHY 6:8–12

Are you, or is someone you know, so beset by greed that you have the terrible feeling that no matter what you do you can never have quite enough? If this is what you are suffering from, understand that you lack not physical possessions but spiritual light:

Ye have sown much, and bring in little; ye eat, but ye have not enough; ye drink, but ye are not filled with

drink; ye clothe you, but there is none warm; and he
that earneth wages earneth wages to put it into a bag
with holes.

Thus saith the Lord of hosts; Consider your ways.

HAGGAI 1:6–7

Perhaps the very next time you yearn for a new possession you will remember the words of Paul that he spoke
to the church elders at Ephesus:

I have showed you all things, how that so laboring ye
ought to support the weak, and to remember the words
of the Lord Jesus, how he said, it is more blessed to give
than to receive.

ACTS 20:35

Giving of yourself, of your earthly possessions, will help
you to understand that what you really need and yearn for
is the love of Jesus Christ. It is His gift of love that will
make you truly rich:

Then Peter said unto them, Repent, and be baptized
every one of you in the name of Jesus Christ for the
remission of sins, and ye shall receive the gift of the
Holy Ghost.

ACTS 2:38

Set your affection on things above, not on things on
the earth.

COLOSSIANS 3:2

The Bible counsels us to think of others, not only of
ourselves. Recognizing the importance of sharing can be
an important antidote to the sin of greed. Remember, too,
past times when you may not have had as much as you do
now, and help others less fortunate than yourselves:

When thou cuttest down thine harvest in thy field, and
hast forgot a sheaf in the field, thou shalt not go again

to fetch it: it shall be for the stranger, for the fatherless, and for the widow: that the Lord thy God may bless thee in all the work of thine hands.

When thou beatest thine olive tree, thou shalt not go over the boughs again: it shall be for the stranger, for the fatherless, and for the widow.

When thou gatherest the grapes of thy vineyard, thou shalt not glean it afterwards: it shall be for the stranger, for the fatherless, and for the widow.

And thou shalt remember that thou wast a bondman in the land of Egypt: therefore I command thee to do this thing.

DEUTERONOMY 24:19–22

Instead of a desire for wealth on this earth, try to cultivate a desire for spiritual wealth. As the beloved Son of God Himself reminds us:

For what shall it profit a man, if he shall gain the whole world, and lose his own soul?

MARK 8:36

And do not think that you can divide your heart and soul. Your allegiance must be to God the Father, and His Son:

Be not deceived; God is not mocked: for whatsoever a man soweth, that shall he also reap.

For he that soweth to his flesh shall of the flesh reap corruption; but he that soweth to the Spirit shall of the Spirit reap life everlasting.

GALATIANS 6:7–8

No man can serve two masters: for either he will hate the one, and love the other; or else he will hold to the one, and despise the other. Ye cannot serve God and mammon.

MATTHEW 6:24

As you turn for help to our Saviour, you will begin to understand that true wealth lies in the riches amassed in the soul, the heart, and the mind:

> Receive my instruction, and not silver; and knowledge rather than choice gold.
> For wisdom is better than rubies; and all the things that may be desired are not to be compared to it.
>
> PROVERBS 8:10–11

As the Bible tells us, if we follow the path of true wisdom, always seeking our spiritual union with God and His Son, we will become rich beyond the dreams of earthly greed:

> Counsel is mine, and sound wisdom: I am understanding; I have strength.
> By me kings reign, and princes decree justice.
> By me princes rule, and nobles, even all the judges of the earth.
> I love them that love me; and those that seek me early shall find me.
> Riches and honor are with me; yea, durable riches and righteousness.
> My fruit is better than gold, yea, than fine gold; and my revenue than choice silver.
> I lead in the way of righteousness, in the midst of the paths of judgment:
> That I may cause those that love me to inherit substance; and I will fill their treasures.
>
> PROVERBS 8:14–21

In your heart of hearts, do you admit that you are greedy, not for wealth but for recognition? You can be helped by the lesson of humility Jesus taught His disciples in Capernaum:

> And he came to Capernaum: and being in the house he asked them, What was it that ye disputed among yourselves by the way?

But they held their peace: for by the way they had disputed among themselves, who should be the greatest.

And he sat down, and called the twelve, and saith unto them, If any man desire to be first, the same shall be last of all, and servant of all.

MARK 9:33-35

With the help of the blessed Saviour, you can substitute a spirit of generosity for greed. In time, the wish for physical possessions will diminish, and you will be happiest when you are sharing what you own, and helping others:

The liberal soul shall be made fat: and he that watereth shall be watered also himself.

He that withholdeth corn, the people shall curse him: but blessing shall be upon the head of him that selleth it.

PROVERBS 11:25-26

The Bible counsels us that the very things we thought would make us most happy on this earth might hold us back from reaching the Kingdom of Heaven. Remember Jesus' words to the man of Judaea who hoped for eternal life:

And when he was gone forth into the way, there came one running, and kneeled to him, and asked him, Good Master, what shall I do that I may inherit eternal life?

And Jesus said unto him, Why callest thou me good? There is none good but one, that is, God.

Thou knowest the commandments, Do not commit adultery, Do not kill, Do not steal, Do not bear false witness, Defraud not, Honor thy father and mother.

And he answered and said unto him, Master, all these have I observed from my youth.

Then Jesus beholding him loved him, and said unto him, One thing thou lackest: go thy way, sell whatsoever thou hast, and give to the poor, and thou shalt have treasure in heaven: and come, take up the cross, and follow me.

And he was sad at that saying, and went away grieved: for he had great possessions.

And Jesus looked round about, and saith unto his disciples, How hardly shall they that have riches enter into the kingdom of God!

And the disciples were astonished at his words. But Jesus answereth again, and saith unto them, Children, how hard is it for them that trust in riches to enter into the Kingdom of God!

It is easier for a camel to go through the eye of a needle, than for a rich man to enter into the kingdom of God.

MARK 10:17-25

The very next time you feel those unwelcome pangs of greed, remember the words of Jesus, and instead of wanting more possessions, do as He advised: take up the cross and follow Him in giving.

Homelessness

It is terrible to be without a home, to be a wanderer, to feel that there is no special place where you can be welcomed, accepted, and loved.

In truth, there are many ways that one can be homeless. A man can own a beautiful house, but yet, if that house is empty of the spirit and the love of God, that house is not really a home, and he will feel homeless.

Perhaps your sense of homelessness is rooted in the knowledge that there is no special place where you are loved or wanted; or your homelessness may be based on the hollow feeling within your soul, indicating that you are empty of the true Spirit of our Saviour.

Whatever has caused your homelessness, the Bible offers you much hope as it tells of others, like yourself, who were wanderers, but who were brought to their true, spiritual homes through the love of God and His beloved Son.

> And the child grew, and was weaned: and Abraham made a great feast the same day that Isaac was weaned.
> And Sarah saw the son of Hagar the Egyptian, which she had born unto Abraham, mocking.
> Wherefore she said unto Abraham, Cast out this bondwoman and her son: for the son of this bondwoman shall not be heir with my son, even with Isaac.
>
> GENESIS 21:8–10

> And God said unto Abraham, Let it not be grievous in thy sight because of the lad, and because of thy bond-

woman; in all that Sarah hath said unto thee, hearken unto her voice; for in Isaac shall thy seed be called.

And also of the son of the bondwoman will I make a nation, because he is thy seed.

GENESIS 21:12–13

The Bible states very clearly that God forgets none of His children. The son of Abraham and his bondwoman, Hagar, was as dear to him as the son of Abraham and Sarah:

> And Abraham rose up early in the morning, and took bread, and a bottle of water, and gave it unto Hagar, putting it on her shoulder, and the child, and sent her away: and she departed, and wandered in the wilderness of Beersheba.
>
> And the water was spent in the bottle, and she cast the child under one of the shrubs.
>
> And she went, and sat her down over against him a good way off, as it were a bowshot: for she said, Let me not see the death of the child. And she sat over against him, and lift up her voice, and wept.
>
> And God heard the voice of the lad; and the angel of God called to Hagar out of heaven, and said unto her, What aileth thee, Hagar? Fear not; for God hath heard the voice of the lad where he is.
>
> Arise, lift up the lad, and hold him in thine hand; for I will make him a great nation.
>
> And God opened her eyes, and she saw a well of water; and she went, and filled the bottle with water, and gave the lad drink.

GENESIS 21:14–19

God wants none of His children to wander in the desert, alone, homeless. As His Angel brought water to Hagar's son, so our Saviour offers you His everlasting love to comfort you when you feel homeless.

Do you need further proof of how God watches over

all of us, and wants none of us to feel abandoned from His love? Here is the story of Jephthah, who was turned out of his home:

> Now Jephthah the Gileadite was a mighty man of valor, and he was the son of a harlot: and Gilead begat Jephthah.
>
> And Gilead's wife bare him sons; and his wife's sons grew up, and they thrust out Jephthah, and said unto him, Thou shalt not inherit in our father's house; for thou art the son of a strange woman.
>
> Then Jephthah fled from his brethren, and dwelt in the land of Tob: and there were gathered vain men to Jephthah, and went out with him.
>
> JUDGES 11:1–3

But though Jephthah was banished from his home, it was to him that the elders of Gilead turned when they were attacked by the children of Ammon, and it was Jephthah who became their chieftain:

> And Jephthah said unto the elders of Gilead, Did not ye hate me, and expel me out of my father's house? and why are ye come unto me now when ye are in distress?
>
> And the elders of Gilead said unto Jephthah, Therefore we turn again to thee now, that thou mayest go with us and fight against the children of Ammon, and be our head over all the inhabitants of Gilead.
>
> And Jephthah said unto the elders of Gilead, If ye bring me home again to fight against the children of Ammon, and the Lord deliver them before me, shall I be your head?
>
> And the elders of Gilead said unto Jephthah, The Lord be witness between us, if we do not so according to thy words.
>
> Then Jephthah went with the elders of Gilead, and the people made him head and captain over them: and Jephthah uttered all his words before the Lord in Mizpeh.
>
> JUDGES 11:7–11

In recent years, the term *displaced people* has become familiar to all of us, but the Bible offers historical proof that people and nations were displaced and made homeless long before our time:

> By the rivers of Babylon, there we sat down, yea, we wept, when we remembered Zion.
>
> We hanged our harps upon the willows in the midst thereof.
>
> For there they that carried us away captive required of us a song; and they that wasted us required of us mirth, saying, Sing us one of the songs of Zion.
>
> How shall we sing the Lord's song in a strange land?
>
> If I forget thee, O Jerusalem, let my right hand forget her cunning.
>
> If I do not remember thee, let my tongue cleave to the roof of my mouth; if I prefer not Jerusalem above my chief joy.
>
> PSALMS 137:1–6

The next time you are afflicted by a terrible sense of homelessness, remember those who were taken captive, and made to sing of their native homeland to their captors. And remember, too, that as God redeemed His people, and returned them to their home, so your homeless spirit can be redeemed by the love of Jesus Christ:

> The wilderness and the solitary place shall be glad for them; and the desert shall rejoice, and blossom as the rose.
>
> It shall blossom abundantly, and rejoice even with joy and singing: the glory of Lebanon shall be given unto it, the excellency of Carmel and Sharon; they shall see the glory of the Lord, and the excellency of our God.
>
> Strengthen ye the weak hands, and confirm the feeble knees.
>
> Say to them that are of a fearful heart, Be strong, fear not: behold, your God will come with vengeance, even God with a recompense; he will come and save you.

Then the eyes of the blind shall be opened, and the ears of the deaf shall be unstopped.

Then shall the lame man leap as a hart, and the tongue of the dumb sing: for in the wilderness shall waters break out, and streams in the desert.

And the parched ground shall become a pool, and the thirsty land springs of water: in the habitation of dragons, where each lay, shall be grass with reeds and rushes.

And a highway shall be there, and a way, and it shall be called The way of holiness; the unclean shall not pass over it; but it shall be for those: the wayfaring men, though fools, shall not err therein.

No lion shall be there, nor any ravenous beast shall go up thereon, it shall not be found there; but the redeemed shall walk there:

And the ransomed of the Lord shall return, and come to Zion with songs and everlasting joy upon their heads: they shall obtain joy and gladness, and sorrow and sighing shall flee away.

ISAIAH 35:1–10

Just as God returned His children to their home where they were happy once again, so His Son can show us the way to our true home, where we will dwell with Him forever:

For we know that if our earthly house of this tabernacle were dissolved, we have a building of God, a house not made with hands, eternal in the heavens.

II CORINTHIANS 5:1

The miracle of the Bible is that we can see today that the promises made ages ago are being kept at this very minute:

And he gave Joshua the son of Nun a charge, and said, Be strong and of a good courage: for thou shalt bring the children of Israel into the land which I sware unto them: and I will be with thee.

DEUTERONOMY 31:23

The word that came to Jeremiah from the Lord, saying,

Thus speaketh the Lord God of Israel, saying, Write thee all the words that I have spoken unto thee in a book.

For, lo, the days come, saith the Lord, that I will bring again the captivity of my people Israel and Judah, saith the Lord: and I will cause them to return to the land that I gave to their fathers, and they shall possess it.

JEREMIAH 30:1–3

If anyone needed proof, here it is, twentieth-century, historical proof that God forgets none of His promises. None of His children will remain homeless forever, as long as they understand that the possessions they must carry with them in their travels is faith:

By faith Abraham, when he was called to go out into a place which he should after receive for an inheritance, obeyed; and he went out, not knowing whither he went.

By faith he sojourned in the land of promise, as in a strange country, dwelling in tabernacles with Isaac and Jacob, the heirs with him of the same promise:

For he looked for a city which hath foundations, whose builder and maker is God.

HEBREWS 11:8–10

And remember, that if you have a spiritual home, you will never feel homeless again. It is the knowledge of the beautiful home that has been prepared for you by our Lord and His beloved Son that will give you a true sense of peace, and the ability to cope with daily problems:

These all died in faith, not having received the promises, but having seen them afar off, and were persuaded of them, and embraced them, and confessed that they were strangers and pilgrims on the earth.

For they that say such things declare plainly that they seek a country.

And truly, if they had been mindful of that country

from whence they came out, they might have had opportunity to have returned.

But now they desire a better country, that is, a heavenly: wherefore God is not ashamed to be called their God: for he hath prepared for them a city.

HEBREWS 11:13–16

We are all pilgrims here on earth, searching for a home in this world, even as we journey toward our home in Heaven, and God is mindful of the prayers of the homeless.

Be comforted, knowing that what He has done for others, He will do for you:

They wandered in the wilderness in a solitary way; they found no city to dwell in.

Hungry and thirsty, their soul fainteth in them.

Then they cried unto the Lord in their trouble, and he delivered them out of their distresses.

And he led them forth by the right way that they might go to a city of habitation.

Oh that men would praise the Lord for his goodness, and for his wonderful works to the children of men!

For he satisfieth the longing soul, and filleth the hungry soul with goodness.

PSALMS 107:4–9

Again the word of the Lord came unto me, saying,

Son of man, thy brethren, even thy brethren, the men of thy kindred, and all the house of Israel wholly, are they unto whom the inhabitants of Jerusalem have said, Get you far from the Lord: unto us is this land given in possession.

Therefore say, Thus saith the Lord God; Although I have cast them far off among the heathen, and although I have scattered them among the countries, yet will I be to them as a little sanctuary in the countries where they shall come.

Therefore say, Thus saith the Lord God; I will even gather you from the people, and assemble you out of the countries where ye have been scattered, and I will give you the land of Israel.

EZEKIEL 11:14–17

No one is ever truly homeless if he travels with God in his heart and Jesus Christ in his spirit.

The next time you feel as though you have no home, remember the story of Ruth who was early left a widow, and who spoke so memorably to her beloved mother-in-law. Cannot the same words and thoughts apply to you and your relationship to God the Father and His Son?

> And Ruth said, Entreat me not to leave thee, or to return from following after thee: for whither thou goest, I will go; and where thou lodgest, I will lodge: thy people shall be my people, and thy God my God:
>
> Where thou diest, will I die, and there will I be buried: the Lord do so to me, and more also, if ought but death part thee and me.

RUTH 1:16–17

Ruth was faithful to her mother-in-law, and she was rewarded with a loving home. If you are as faithful to the Son of God, you will be rewarded by finding peace with Him, and you will never again be troubled by spiritual homelessness:

> Then Peter began to say unto him, Lo, we have left all, and have followed thee.
>
> And Jesus answered and said, Verily I say unto you, There is no man that hath left house, or brethren, or sisters, or father, or mother, or wife, or children, or lands, for my sake, and the gospel's,
>
> But he shall receive a hundredfold now in this time, houses, and brethren, and sisters, and mothers, and children, and lands, with persecutions; and in the world to come eternal life.
>
> But many that are first shall be last; and the last first.

MARK 10:28–31

Hopelessness

If life offers you the tiniest bit of hope, you can go on. There is something to look forward to, a reasonable feeling that tomorrow or possibly the day after will be better.

But what of those times when, as author John Bunyan wrote in *Pilgrim's Progress,* you reach the slough of despond, and you see before you a gloomy building which Bunyan called, "Doubting Castle," which, he said, was owned by the "Giant Despair."

No one can function well if his life is filled with despondency, doubt, and despair. It is these emotions that lead one to the still-blacker emotion of hopelessness.

The very first thing to do when beset on all sides by the dragons of hopelessness is to remember that you are not alone, that you stand with God the Father on one side of you, and His beloved Son on the other. Take a deep breath, inhale God's air, read the following; if you can, memorize the words:

> My sheep hear my voice, and I know them, and they follow me:
> And I give unto them eternal life; and they shall never perish, neither shall any man pluck them out of my hand.
> My Father, which gave them to me, is greater than all; and no man is able to pluck them out of my Father's hand.
> I and my Father are one.
>
> JOHN 10:27–30

How can you feel completely hopeless when you know that you are in the loving embrace of our Saviour? But

perhaps, even as you read this, you say that no one can
possibly understand your problems, or what you are suffering. No one has gone through such travail as you are
now experiencing. But the Bible is here to point out to
you that you are not alone in your suffering. Job knew
such hopelessness that he actually prayed that his life
might end:

> Oh that I might have my request; and that God would
> grant me the thing that I long for!
>
> Even that it would please God to destroy me; that he
> would let loose his hand, and cut me off!
>
> Then should I yet have comfort; yea, I would harden
> myself in sorrow: let him not spare; for I have not con-
> cealed the words of the Holy One.
>
> What is my strength, that I should hope? And what is
> mine end, that I should prolong my life?
>
> Is my strength the strength of stones? Or is my flesh of
> brass?
>
> Is not my help in me? And is wisdom driven quite
> from me?
>
> JOB 6:8–13

Job's despair was so all encompassing that he raised his
voice up, and asked where he might find hope:

> My days are past, my purposes are broken off, even the
> thoughts of my heart.
>
> They change the night into day: the light is short be-
> cause of darkness.
>
> If I wait, the grave is mine house: I have made my bed
> in the darkness.
>
> I have said to corruption, Thou art my father: to the
> worm, Thou art my mother, and my sister.
>
> And where is now my hope? As for my hope, who shall
> see it?
>
> JOB 17:11–15

And as Job questioned where he might find hope, he
also longed to come closer to God, because he felt that it

was not within any man's province to understand God's ways; even though he was in despair, he remained faithful to the One on High.

After all his trials and tribulations, Job's faithfulness was rewarded; God blessed Job with twice as much as he had before:

> And in all the land were no women found so fair as the daughters of Job: and their father gave them inheritance among their brethren.
> After this lived Job a hundred and forty years, and saw his sons, and his sons' sons, even four generations.
> So Job died, being old and full of days.
>
> JOB 42:15–17

The Good Book makes it clear that in the darkest hour there is hope for you. Even if you have sinned, do not give up hope that you can be forgiven:

> But the scripture hath concluded all under sin, that the promise by faith of Jesus Christ might be given to them that believe.
>
> GALATIANS 3:22

What can drive out hopelessness? The twin healers: Faith and Belief. Jesus can save all those whose hearts are open to Him:

> And a certain woman named Lydia, a seller of purple, of the city of Thyatira, which worshipped God, heard us: whose heart the Lord opened, that she attended unto the things which were spoken of Paul.
>
> ACTS 16:14

Certainly anyone whose heart has been opened can feel that greatest hope of all, the hope of salvation. God and Jesus ask nothing more of you than that you come close to Them:

Draw nigh to God, and he will draw nigh to you.
Cleanse your hands, ye sinners; and purify your hearts,
ye double minded.

JAMES 4:8

There is hope for all who are honest with God and
Jesus, and with themselves. For what is the purpose of ad-
mitting sinfulness to others if you don't truly believe in
what you are saying? You may be able to fool your friends,
but it is certainly not possible to fool God:

For what is the hope of the hypocrite, though he hath
gained, when God taketh away his soul?

JOB 27:8

Perhaps your feelings of hopelessness are not based so
much on the lack in your soul, but in the circumstances
that surround you—circumstances you seem powerless to
change. It is true that most of us are very often powerless:
we are in the grip of earth-shaking events that we cannot
control. But remember that there is One who is all-
knowledgeable and all-powerful. Turn to Him for help:

He will swallow up death in victory; and the Lord God
will wipe away tears from off all faces; and the rebuke of
his people shall he take away from off all the earth: for
the Lord hath spoken it.

And it shall be said in that day, Lo, this is our God;
we have waited for him, and he will save us: this is the
Lord; we have waited for him, we will be glad and rejoice in his salvation.

ISAIAH 25:8-9

As hope returns to you, remember not to despair so
easily the next time you are afflicted by troubles or doubts.
Think of Abraham who founded a great nation, because
he never stopped believing in the possibility of God's
miracle:

Who against hope believed in hope, that he might become the father of many nations, according to that which was spoken, So shall thy seed be.

ROMANS 4:18

There is that old saying that the sky is darkest just before the arrival of dawn, and our souls are also experiencing their darkest, most hopeless hour until the arrival of faith. Then, suddenly, we are in the midst of a glorious morning:

Arise, shine; for thy light is come, and the glory of the Lord is risen upon thee.

For, behold, the darkness shall cover the earth, and gross darkness the people: but the Lord shall arise upon thee, and his glory shall be seen upon thee.

ISAIAH 60:1–2

Don't be wary of the hope, the joy, that you feel suddenly springing to life within you. God has always wanted His children to serve Him joyously, and don't think that the kindness He is offering will be removed from you.

Allow the hope you're feeling at this very moment to blossom and grow, even as you remember that God's promise to Noah is really God's promise to all of us:

For this is as the waters of Noah unto me: for as I have sworn that the waters of Noah should no more go over the earth; so have I sworn that I would not be wroth with thee, nor rebuke thee.

For the mountains shall depart, and the hills be removed; but my kindness shall not depart from thee, neither shall the covenant of my peace be removed, saith the Lord that hath mercy on thee.

O thou afflicted, tossed with tempest, and not comforted, behold, I will lay thy stones with fair colors, and lay thy foundations with sapphires.

And I will make thy windows of agates, and thy gates of carbuncles, and all thy borders of pleasant stones.

And all thy children shall be taught of the Lord; and great shall be the peace of thy children.

ISAIAH 54:9–13

There is so much within the Scriptures that can renew our hope:

When thou passest through the waters, I will be with thee; and through the rivers, they shall not overflow thee: when thou walkest through the fire, thou shalt not be burned; neither shall the flame kindle upon thee.

ISAIAH 43:2

And most wonderful of all is the hope brought to us by our Redeemer and Saviour, Jesus Christ. He has told us that He is the bread of life, and whoever comes to Him with an open heart that is ready to be filled with faith and belief will know life everlasting.

Read the following, and you will never again succumb to hopelessness:

And Jesus said unto them, I am the bread of life: he that cometh to me shall never hunger; and he that believeth on me shall never thirst.

JOHN 6:35

And this is the will of him that sent me, that every one which seeth the Son, and believeth on him, may have everlasting life: and I will raise him up at the last day.

JOHN 6:40

He requires so very little of us, and He is eager to give us so very much. The very thought that Christ feels that we are worthy of his love should fill us with the hope spoken about by Peter:

Wherefore gird up the loins of your mind, be sober, and hope to the end for the grace that is to be brought unto you at the revelation of Jesus Christ.

I PETER 1:13

Remember, too, that very often the thing we most hope for—eternal life—is not something we can see; it is not a physical possession that we can touch, turn around in our hands, or hold up to a lamp. Eternal life can be visualized only if we hold it high and examine it beneath the brightest light of all—the light of faith:

For we are saved by hope: but hope that is seen is not hope: for what a man seeth, why doth he yet hope for?
For if we hope for that we see not, then do we with patience wait for it.

ROMANS 8:24–25

Feeling hopeless? Rid yourself of that burden forever! How can any of us who have found salvation in our Lord Jesus feel hopeless? We know He is ever with us, loving us, caring for us, promising that we shall abide with Him. Surely, that should imbue us with hope no matter how many times we may be troubled:

For what is our hope, or joy, or crown of rejoicing? Are not even ye in the presence of our Lord Jesus Christ at his coming?
For ye are our glory and joy.

I THESSALONIANS 2:19–20

The next time you find yourself thinking either, I feel hopeless, or I am hopeless, find yourself a quiet corner and sit down. Take the Bible in your hand and read aloud:

The Lord is my shepherd; I shall not want.
He maketh me to lie down in green pastures: he leadeth me beside the still waters.

He restoreth my soul: he leadeth me in the paths of righteousness for his name's sake.

Yea, though I walk through the valley of the shadow of death, I will fear no evil: for thou art with me; thy rod and thy staff they comfort me.

Thou preparest a table before me in the presence of mine enemies: thou anointest my head with oil; my cup runneth over.

Surely goodness and mercy shall follow me all the days of my life: and I will dwell in the house of the Lord for ever.

PSALMS 23:1–6

There it is, vivid proof of how very much the Lord loves you. Surely, you cannot feel hopeless about your life, your future, or your soul once you know that!

Hostility

Hostility is a terrible, double-edged sword. How can the person who experiences your hostility respond but with a hostility of his own? And how do you react when someone is hostile toward you—again, with hostility. Hostility feeds upon itself, building terrible temples of hate.

These temples must be torn down, and this can only be accomplished by turning from hostility, rather than adding to it. Naturally, none of us is so saintly that we can entirely avoid feelings of hostility when we are sure that someone has wronged us. But we must try to cultivate the feelings of brotherly love within us, because in time this love will drive the hostility from our hearts and minds.

> He therefore that despiseth, despiseth not man, but God, who hath also given us his holy Spirit.
> But as touching brotherly love ye need not that I write unto you: for ye yourselves are taught of God to love one another.
>
> I THESSALONIANS 4:8–9

The Scriptures, which represent the constant and enduring Word of God, tell us, instruct us, beseech us to love one another, as we would be loved by our Lord and His beloved Son. If we respond to all these pleas with antagonism, we are not only hurting ourselves, but we also are going against the Word of God:

Beloved, let us love one another: for love is of God; and every one that loveth is born of God, and knoweth God.

He that loveth not knoweth not God; for God is love.

I JOHN 4:7–8

Try to conquer hostility with love. Not to do so is a terrible rejection of God and the offering He made to us of His Son:

In this was manifested the love of God toward us, because that God sent his only begotten Son into the world, that we might live through him.

Herein is love, not that we loved God, but that he loved us, and sent his Son to be the propitiation for our sins.

Beloved, if God so loved us, we ought also to love one another.

No man hath seen God at any time. If we love one another, God dwelleth in us, and his love is perfected in us.

I JOHN 4:9–12

Perhaps you are thinking that only the Divine Son of God can return love for hate and hostility. It is not within us to emulate such perfection. Naturally, we can never be as perfect as Lord Jesus, but we can try to follow His example.

Certainly the greatest example of wicked hostility was when Jesus was brought to Calvary. Yet, how did Jesus reply to His tormentors?

And when they were come to the place, which is called Calvary, there they crucified him, and the malefactors, one on the right hand, and the other on the left.

Then said Jesus, Father, forgive them; for they know not what they do. And they parted his raiment, and cast lots.

LUKE 23:33–34

As we are children of Jesus and He is always with us, we must always try to keep His examples before us and remember His teachings:

> For where two or three are gathered together in my name, there am I in the midst of them.
> Then came Peter to him, and said, Lord, how oft shall my brother sin against me, and I forgive him? Till seven times?
> Jesus saith unto him, I say not unto thee, Until seven times: but, Until seventy times seven.
>
> MATTHEW 18:20–22

Picture the world if everyone forgave their enemies—wouldn't it be a wonderful place? You cannot dictate behavior to the entire world, but you can do your best to lessen hostility around you. Every time you do so, you add evidence that the sacrifice of the Lamb of God was not in vain.

Remember His words when He spoke from the mountain top:

> Blessed are the peacemakers: for they shall be called the children of God.
>
> MATTHEW 5:9

Returning love for hostility, giving more good things than are asked for, that is our Saviour's constant plea to all who would heed Him:

> Ye have heard that it hath been said, An eye for an eye, and a tooth for a tooth:
> But I say unto you, That ye resist not evil: but whosoever shall smite thee on thy right cheek, turn to him the other also.
> And if any man will sue thee at the law, and take away thy coat, let him have thy cloak also.

And whosoever shall compel thee to go a mile, go with him twain.

MATTHEW 5:38–41

Do you ever feel hostile toward others for no apparent reason? This sort of deep, unreasoning antagonism is a true illness of the soul, and you are harming yourself most of all:

For all the law is fulfilled in one word, even in this; Thou shalt love thy neighbor as thyself.
But if ye bite and devour one another, take heed that ye be not consumed one of another.

GALATIANS 5:14–15

To temper the hostility within your soul, think of this key word: Forgiveness.

Our Lord Jesus Christ forgave His enemies; He forgives us every day if we come to Him repentant and asking for His help. Let us try to be as forgiving, as charitable, toward others:

Put on therefore, as the elect of God, holy and beloved, bowels of mercies, kindness, humbleness of mind, meekness, long-suffering.
Forbearing one another, and forgiving one another, if any man have a quarrel against any: even as Christ forgave you, so also do ye.
And above all these things put on charity, which is the bond of perfectness.
And let the peace of God rule in your hearts, to the which also ye are called in one body; and ye be thankful.

COLOSSIANS 3:12–15

Is it possible to change an enemy into a friend? All things are possible when done in the name of Christ. One way is to empathize, to try to understand what the other person is enduring that makes him so hostile toward you.

As the poet Henry Wadsworth Longfellow said, "If we could read the secret history of our enemies, we should find in each man's life sorrow and suffering enough to disarm all hostility."

The next time someone behaves in a hostile manner toward you, ask yourself, Is this person angry with me about something I've done? Or is he, in truth, angry with himself about something he has done, and is this his reason for becoming offensive? After you've thought about that, continue in thoughtfulness, and ask, Is this person angry with me, or is he suffering other troubles? Is there illness in his family? Is he worried about his job? Is he afraid of the future?

You may discover that this man's hostility is misdirected and stems from fear rather than from any real antagonism toward you. Armed with this knowledge, you can afford to be generous and do as the Bible advises:

> Ye have heard that it hath been said, Thou shalt love thy neighbor, and hate thine enemy.
>
> But I say unto you, Love your enemies, bless them that curse you, do good to them that hate you, and pray for them which despitefully use you, and persecute you;
>
> That ye may be the children of your Father which is in heaven: for he maketh his sun to rise on the evil and on the good, and sendeth rain on the just and on the unjust.
>
> MATTHEW 5:43–45

Possibly you feel that you cannot live up to all that is required of you. But all things are possible if you pray to God for strength, and pray to Jesus Christ for compassion.

Do not say that you will limit your loving kindness to those who love you. There's nothing difficult about returning love, but to be truly worthy of our Saviour's sacrifice, you must at least try to care about those who don't seem to be very caring of you. And quite possibly, your tenderness may generate a like emotion in others:

> For if ye love them which love you, what reward have ye? Do not even the publicans the same?
>
> And if ye salute your brethren only, what do ye more than others? Do not even the publicans so?
>
> Be ye therefore perfect, even as your Father which is in heaven is perfect.
>
> MATTHEW 5:46–48

You can look forward to great happiness once you have managed to root hostility out of your life:

> Behold, how good and how pleasant it is for brethren to dwell together in unity!
>
> PSALMS 133:1

> But love ye your enemies, and do good, and lend, hoping for nothing again; and your reward shall be great, and ye shall be the children of the Highest: for he is kind unto the unthankful and to the evil.
>
> Be ye therefore merciful, as your Father also is merciful.
>
> LUKE 6:35–36

The very next time you are faced with hostility, do not meet it head-on with still more antagonism. Instead, put your hand out to your troubled brother, and do your best to help him:

> Now we exhort you, brethren, warn them that are unruly, comfort the feeble-minded, support the weak, be patient toward all men.
>
> See that none render evil for evil unto any man; but ever follow that which is good, both among yourselves, and to all men.
>
> I THESSALONIANS 5:14–15

Try to think of yourself always as a messenger of Jesus Christ. You are following His Word, and you want to bring news of the same Word to others:

> And I thank Christ Jesus our Lord, who hath enabled me, for that he counted me faithful, putting me into the ministry.
>
> I TIMOTHY 1:12

The message that you are trying to deliver is that love is more important than hate, and forgiveness more valuable than hostility:

> And when ye stand praying, forgive, if ye have ought against any: that your Father also which is in heaven may forgive you your trespasses.
> But if ye do not forgive, neither will your Father which is in heaven forgive your trespasses.
>
> MARK 11:25–26

In time, you can look forward to the marvelous peace that comes to the heart which knows no anger, and the soul which is foreign to hostility.

Just as nations who are at peace with one another live side by side in amity, so you will enjoy a happier relationship with the people who are part of your life:

> And he shall judge among the nations, and shall rebuke many people: and they shall beat their swords into plowshares, and their spears into pruninghooks: nation shall not lift up sword against nation, neither shall they learn war any more.
>
> ISAIAH 2:4

Insecurity

All of us experience insecurity from time to time. We feel that we're not good enough, or that our accomplishments are few, or valueless.

Sometimes we're sure that we can't measure up to all that is required of us, other times we are sure that not even those closest to us really care about us. On really bad days, we can't stop questioning our own worth over and over again.

Insecurity is a common affliction. Indeed, a certain measure of insecurity can be useful. People who never question their own thoughts or actions, who feel that everything they do is right and perfect, are the truly unpleasant people of this world. These people are imbued with egos so large that they are completely insensitive to the world around them, or to the opinions of other people.

Some insecurity, as it is expressed in a questioning of our own worth and values, is a good thing. It means that we are aware of our own imperfections and the need we all have to improve. However, when insecurity looms so large that it stops us from carrying out important actions, and from living full, healthy lives, we must consider the depth and reasons for this paralyzing bulk of insecurity.

Let the Bible help you examine the reasons for your heavy feelings of insecurity. You can arrive at a better understanding of yourself, and an important belief that you are a person worthy of Christ's love.

Perhaps your greatest area of insecurity stems from a feeling that you are not lovable, and therefore no one loves you. However, you know that this is not really true; the most important One of all does love you, and you are a part of Him. How can you feel loveless, when He has said:

> Abide in me, and I in you. As the branch cannot bear fruit of itself, except it abide in the vine; no more can ye, except ye abide in me.
>
> I am the vine, ye are the branches: He that abideth in me, and I in him, the same bringeth forth much fruit: for without me ye can do nothing.
>
> If a man abide not in me, he is cast forth as a branch, and is withered; and men gather them, and cast them into the fire, and they are burned.
>
> If ye abide in me, and my words abide in you, ye shall ask what ye will, and it shall be done unto you.
>
> Herein is my Father glorified, that ye bear much fruit; so shall ye be my disciples.
>
> As the Father hath loved me, so have I loved you: continue ye in my love.
>
> JOHN 15:4–9

Not only does God's beloved Son love you, but because you have reciprocated that love, our Heavenly Father offers you love, too:

> For the Father himself loveth you, because ye have loved me, and have believed that I came out from God.
>
> JOHN 16:27

It is clear, then, that if you are worthy to receive the love of God the Father, and God the Son, you are also worthy of the love around you. This is especially true if you continue to reach out to our Saviour:

> But grow in grace, and in the knowledge of our Lord and Saviour Jesus Christ. To him be glory both now and for ever. Amen.
>
> II PETER 3:18

Perhaps your extreme feelings of insecurity stem from feelings of guilt. However, the Book tells us over and over again that only God has the right to judge, and only God may condemn.

If you feel guilty about something you have done, and if you are truly repentant, both God and His Son will allow you to come to Them again:

> Jesus went unto the Mount of Olives.
>
> And early in the morning he came again into the temple, and all the people came unto him; and he sat down, and taught them.
>
> And the scribes and Pharisees brought unto him a woman taken in adultery; and when they had set her in the midst,
>
> They said unto him, Master, this woman was taken in adultery, in the very act.
>
> Now Moses in the law commanded us, that such should be stoned: but what sayest thou?
>
> This they said, tempting him, that they might have to accuse him. But Jesus stooped down, and with his finger wrote on the ground, as though he heard them not.
>
> So when they continued asking him, he lifted up himself, and said unto them, He that is without sin among you, let him first cast a stone at her.
>
> JOHN 8:1–7

There was no one then—nor is there anyone today— who is completely blameless. And as John tells us, everyone was "convicted by their own conscience," and no stones were cast. Indeed, the men drifted away shamefacedly to their own homes, and the woman was left there alone with Jesus, who asked her if any man had remained to condemn her:

> She said, No man, Lord. And Jesus said unto her, Neither do I condemn thee: go, and sin no more.
>
> JOHN 8:11

Insecurity may also stem from the fact that you are not as wealthy as some of your friends or neighbors. But you must understand that worldly goods, while they may be pleasant enough, are not the important riches that you should possess:

> Charge them that are rich in this world, that they be not high-minded, nor trust in uncertain riches, but in the living God, who giveth us richly all things to enjoy;
> That they do good, that they be rich in good works, ready to distribute, willing to communicate;
> Laying up in store for themselves a good foundation against the time to come, that they may lay hold on eternal life.
>
> I TIMOTHY 6:17–19

Your insecurity will diminish as you realize that you are held in God's hands. Instead of spending hours worrying about who you are, and what you are, be prayerful, and understanding that you are an important person— important to God—who will bring you peace:

> Be careful for nothing; but in every thing by prayer and supplication with thanksgiving let your requests be made known unto God.
> And the peace of God, which passeth all understanding, shall keep your hearts and minds through Christ Jesus.
>
> PHILIPPIANS 4:6–7

As you lay down your burden of excessive insecurity, you will be able to say:

> I will both lay me down in peace, and sleep: for thou, Lord, only makest me dwell in safety.
>
> PSALMS 4:8

When assailed by feelings of insecurity, remind yourself that you are dear to Jesus Christ. Let your acceptance of

Him as our Saviour give you a sense of completeness, a sense of greater self-worth:

> Cast not away therefore your confidence, which hath great recompense of reward.
>
> For ye have need of patience, that, after ye have done the will of God, ye might receive promise.
>
> For yet a little while, and he that shall come will come, and will not tarry.
>
> Now the just shall live by faith: but if any man draw back, my soul shall have no pleasure in him.
>
> But we are not of them who draw back unto perdition; but of them that believe to the saving of the soul.
>
> HEBREWS 10:35–39

Constant anxiety is another symptom suffered by a truly insecure person. There are some anxieties that are based on very real fears. If you are driving your car on an icy road, you are naturally anxious that you may go into a skid. If the bills are piling up, and you are out of a job, you are anxious about how you will find the money to pay your debts.

However, there are other anxieties that stem from feelings of apprehension, helplessness, and discouragement. Possibly you can't explain just why you feel this way, but yet the feelings are painfully real. This anxiety just adds to your already overweening insecurity, and you may think that if you were a worthwhile person you wouldn't be so troubled. You are a very worthwhile person! The Bible, which is God's Word, constantly stresses that you are important, you are loved, you are protected, you are cared for.

Instead of feeling shaky and insecure, come, lean on God:

> Trust in the Lord with all thine heart; and lean not unto thine own understanding.

> In all thy ways acknowledge him, and he shall direct thy paths.
>
> PROVERBS 3:5-6

Unfortunately, there are some people in this world who have not yet found salvation, have not yet come to Jesus Christ. These are the people who might prey on your feelings of insecurity when you are at your weakest. Do not argue or contend with them; instead, take solace from reading the following:

> For the Lord God will help me; therefore shall I not be confounded: therefore have I set my face like flint, and I know that I shall not be ashamed.
> He is near that justifieth me; who will contend with me? Let us stand together: who is mine adversary? Let him come near to me.
> Behold, the Lord God will help me; who is he that shall condemn me? Lo, they all shall wax old as a garment; the moth shall eat them up.
>
> ISAIAH 50:7-9

The person who knows that he is valuable—and you must know that you are very valuable to our Father and His Son—need fear no other person's cruel words:

> Hearken unto me, ye that know righteousness, the people in whose heart is my law; fear ye not the reproach of men, neither be ye afraid of their revilings.
>
> ISAIAH 51:7

Rejection by others can also cause painful feelings of insecurity, but remember, that though people of small minds may reject you for unimportant reasons, you will never be rejected by our Lord, Jesus Christ:

> All that the Father giveth me shall come to me; and him that cometh to me I will in no wise cast out.
>
> JOHN 6:37

Keep reminding yourself that it is not the opinion of others that matters, but the love of God.

The knowledge of the wisest person on this earth is finite and limited, but His wisdom is infinite, and He cares for you:

> The Lord by wisdom hath founded the earth; by understanding hath he established the heavens.
>
> By his knowledge the depths are broken up, and the clouds drop down the dew.
>
> My son, let not them depart from thine eyes: keep sound wisdom and discretion:
>
> So shall they be life unto thy soul, and grace to thy neck.
>
> Then shalt thou walk in thy way safely, and thy foot shall not stumble.
>
> When thou liest down, thou shalt not be afraid: yea, thou shalt lie down, and thy sleep shall be sweet.
>
> Be not afraid of sudden fear, neither of the desolation of the wicked, when it cometh.
>
> For the Lord shall be thy confidence, and shall keep thy foot from being taken.
>
> PROVERBS 3:19–26

As your insecurity diminishes, and your security about your own worth grows, you will become a more open person, ready to accept others more easily. When this happens, the greatest measure of your newfound security will be your desire to do more for others:

> Withhold not good from them to whom it is due, when it is in the power of thine hand to do it.
>
> Say not unto thy neighbor, Go, and come again, and tomorrow I will give; when thou hast it by thee.
>
> Devise not evil against thy neighbor, seeing he dwelleth securely by thee.
>
> Strive not with a man without cause, if he have done thee no harm.

Envy thou not the oppressor, and choose none of his ways.

PROVERBS 3:27–31

The more you do for others, the more accepting they will become of you. The added security you have gained through the loving help of our Lord and our Saviour will fill your days with a new experience of joy.

Remember, always, that your true security is based on your faith.

Loneliness and Desolation

Oh, the pain of loneliness! The feeling that there will never be another person in one's life who will really care. Everyone, at one time or another, has gone through this deep, despairing sense of being completely alone in an uncaring, disinterested world.

This is the time to reach out and take the hand that is always being offered to you, the love that has been waiting patiently for you: the hand and the love of Jesus Christ, our Saviour.

Can you possibly get through another day, another night of loneliness and desolation? If you believe, truly believe, you will come to understand that you are never alone. And once that belief enters your soul, the desolation you now feel will disappear; it will melt away like a winter day's icy snows—it will disappear beneath the bright sun of faith.

> The Lord redeemeth the soul of his servants: and none of them that trust in him shall be desolate.
>
> PSALMS 34:22

The Bible clearly tells of God's promise to man, His word that the man who believes will never be forsaken; indeed, he will be brought to a fair and lovely place.

> Thou shalt no more be termed Forsaken; neither shall thy land any more be termed Desolate: but thou shalt be

called Hephzibah, and thy land Beulah: for the Lord delighteth in thee, and thy land shall be married.

ISAIAH 62:4

Have you committed a sin that you feel is so grievous that you believe yourself to be driven forever from the world of men? Remember, that even though you may not be able to forgive yourself, God has infinite compassion, and He will care for you even as he cared for Cain, the son of Adam and Eve.

Behold, thou hast driven me out this day from the face of the earth; and from thy face shall I be hid; and I shall be a fugitive and a vagabond in the earth; and it shall come to pass, that every one that findeth me shall slay me.

And the Lord said unto him, Therefore whosoever slayeth Cain, vengeance shall be taken on him sevenfold. And the Lord set a mark upon Cain, lest any finding him should kill him.

And Cain went out from the presence of the Lord, and dwelt in the land of Nod, on the east of Eden.

GENESIS 4:14–16

But it is the beloved Son who stands always beside you, forever offering you His love, His pity, His understanding. Read the following, to find help and banish your loneliness:

And Jesus went about all the cities and villages, teaching in their synagogues, and preaching the gospel of the kingdom, and healing every sickness and every disease among the people.

But when he saw the multitudes, he was moved with compassion on them, because they fainted, and were scattered abroad, as sheep having no shepherd.

MATTHEW 9:35–36

And indeed, who could have more compassion for us than our Saviour, who has promised:

Teaching them to observe all things whatsoever I have commanded you: and, lo, I am with you alway, even unto the end of the world. Amen.

MATTHEW 28:20

There is solace in the knowledge that nothing—not the most dire circumstances—can ever separate us from the love of Jesus:

Who shall separate us from the love of Christ? Shall tribulation, or distress, or persecution, or famine, or nakedness, or peril, or sword?

As it is written, For thy sake we are killed all the day long; we are accounted as sheep for the slaughter.

Nay, in all these things we are more than conquerors through him that loved us.

ROMANS 8:35–37

There is no point, when suffering from extreme loneliness, to rush out into a crowd of men. True, you will be among people, but they will not be able to give you the help you can gain from communion with God and His Son. Turn, instead, for comfort to the Psalms:

I looked on my right hand, and beheld, but there was no man that would know me: refuge failed me; no man cared for my soul.

I cried unto thee, O Lord: I said, Thou art my refuge and my portion in the land of the living.

Attend unto my cry; for I am brought very low: deliver me from my persecutors; for they are stronger than I.

PSALMS 142:4–6

It is important to understand that loneliness and desolation are not ills visited only upon you. These feelings have been experienced by men throughout the ages:

He hath put my brethren far from me, and mine acquaintance are verily estranged from me.

My kinsfolk have failed, and my familiar friends have forgotten me.

They that dwell in mine house, and my maids, count me for a stranger: I am an alien in their sight.

JOB 19:13–15

Now the Lord had prepared a great fish to swallow up Jonah. And Jonah was in the belly of the fish three days and three nights.

JONAH 1:17

By night on my bed I sought him whom my soul loveth: I sought him, but I found him not.

I will rise now, and go about the city in the streets, and in the broad ways I will seek him whom my soul loveth: I sought him, but I found him not.

The watchmen that go about the city found me: to whom I said, Saw ye him whom my soul loveth?

SONG OF SOLOMON 3:1–3

How doth the city sit solitary, that was full of people! How is she become as a widow! She that was great among the nations, and princess among the provinces, how is she become tributary!

She weepeth sore in the night, and her tears are on her cheeks: among all her lovers she hath none to comfort her; all her friends have dealt treacherously with her, they are become her enemies.

LAMENTATIONS 1:1–2

I opened to my beloved; but my beloved had withdrawn himself, and was gone: my soul failed when he spake: I sought him, but I could not find him; I called him, but he gave me no answer.

The watchmen that went about the city found me, they smote me, they wounded me; the keepers of the walls took away my veil from me.

SONG OF SOLOMON 5:6–7

But just as the Bible relates the stories of others who have been afflicted with loneliness and desolation, the Good Book also expresses the great hope that may come to all who believe.

Today you are lonely, but take hope, the loneliness will pass. Think of yourself as a child, going to your parents because you have suffered a hurt. In the same way, turn to our Heavenly Father and His Son, and they will comfort you:

> I will not leave you comfortless: I will come to you.
> Yet a little while, and the world seeth me no more; but ye see me: because I live, ye shall live also.
> At that day ye shall know that I am in my Father, and ye in me, and I in you.
>
> JOHN 14:18–20

Take comfort in these words that promise eternal friendship to all those who believe:

> Behold, I stand at the door, and knock: if any man hear my voice, and open the door, I will come in to him, and will sup with him, and he with me.
>
> REVELATION 3:20

Do you live alone? Understand that when you walk into your home there is a Spirit there waiting to welcome you. The loving Spirit of the Saviour who assures us that He is always with us:

> He that regardeth the day, regardeth it unto the Lord; and he that regardeth not the day, to the Lord he doth not regard it. He that eateth, eateth to the Lord, for he giveth God thanks; and he that eateth not, to the Lord he eateth not, and giveth God thanks.
> For none of us liveth to himself, and no man dieth to himself.

For whether we live, we live unto the Lord; and
whether we die, we die unto the Lord; whether we live
therefore, or die, we are the Lord's.

ROMANS 14:6–8

The greatest faith of all was shown by Jesus Christ. He
was able to speak calmly to His disciples. He told them
that though He would be abandoned by men, He knew
that He would never be alone. It is this same faith and trust
you must cultivate if you are to rid yourself of those debilitating feelings of loneliness. The next time you feel as
though there is no one who truly cares for you, remember
the following:

Behold, the hour cometh, yea, is now come, that ye
shall be scattered, every man to his own, and shall leave
me alone: and yet I am not alone, because the Father is
with me.

These things I have spoken unto you, that in me ye
might have peace. In the world ye shall have tribulation:
but be of good cheer; I have overcome the world.

JOHN 16:32–33

Oppression

Why do men insist on oppressing others who could be good friends or good neighbors? Understanding this kind of cruelty is never easy. It is not easy always to turn the other cheek, and all of us, at one time or another, feel that the way to end oppression is to fight against it.

However, this is not a battle that can be fought single-handedly. We need all the help that we can find. Help from others who understand that those who would oppress their fellows stand far from the love of God; but even though we stand a million strong, we are weak if we do not have the Holy Spirit by our side.

The Bible relates many stories of injustice, and it relates, too, the help that was forthcoming from on high— the help that is necessary if the oppressed are to rise and throw off the tyrant's shackles.

> And Joshua said, Hereby ye shall know that the living God is among you, and that he will without fail drive out from before you the Canaanites, and the Hittites, and the Hivites, and the Perizzites, and the Girgashites, and the Amorites, and the Jebusites.
>
> Behold, the ark of the covenant of the Lord of all the earth passeth over before you into Jordan.
>
> JOSHUA 3:10–11

> And it came to pass, when the people removed from their tents, to pass over Jordan, and the priests bearing the ark of the covenant before the people;

And as they that bare the ark were come unto Jordan,
and the feet of the priests that bare the ark were dipped
in the brim of the water, (for Jordan overfloweth all his
banks all the time of harvest,)

That the waters which came down from above stood
and rose up upon a heap very far from the city Adam,
that is beside Zaretan: and those that came down toward
the sea of the plain, even the salt sea, failed, and were
cut off: and the people passed over right against Jericho.

And the priests that bare the ark of the covenant of
the Lord stood firm on dry ground in the midst of
Jordan, and all the Israelites passed over on dry ground,
until all the people were passed clean over Jordan.

JOSHUA 3:14-17

The miracle of Joshua and the parting of the waters of
the Jordan is well-known, and what has been so carefully
documented in the Bible can happen again—today—to
you—to all those who suffer oppression. It is important to
remember where to look for help:

The eternal God is thy refuge, and underneath are the
everlasting arms: and he shall thrust out the enemy from
before thee; and shall say, Destroy them.

DEUTERONOMY 33:27

Those everlasting arms are always held open to you.
Think of them when others trouble you. Ask for a refuge.
Help is closer than you think if you will just pray for it:

The Lord also will be a refuge for the oppressed, a
refuge in times of trouble.

And they that know thy name will put their trust in
thee: for thou, Lord, hast not forsaken them that seek
thee.

Sing praises to the Lord, which dwelleth in Zion: declare among the people his doings.

When he maketh inquisition for blood, he remembereth them: he forgetteth not the cry of the humble.

PSALMS 9:9-12

It is only natural that the oppressor will make you fearful, but take heart and say over and over:

> So that we may boldly say, the Lord is my helper, and I will not fear what man shall do unto me.
>
> HEBREWS 13:6

Remember that our God and our Saviour have a very special place for those who are held in bondage. You can be led from oppression just as the children of Israel were led from Egypt:

> And the Lord said, I have surely seen the affliction of my people which are in Egypt, and have heard their cry by reason of their taskmasters; for I know their sorrows;
>
> And I am come down to deliver them out of the hand of the Egyptians, and to bring them up out of that land unto a good land and a large, unto a land flowing with milk and honey; unto the place of the Canaanites, and the Hittites, and the Amorites, and the Perizzites, and the Hivites, and the Jebusites.
>
> Now therefore, behold, the cry of the children of Israel is come unto me: and I have also seen the oppression wherewith the Egyptians oppress them.
>
> Come now therefore, and I will send thee unto Pharaoh, that thou mayest bring forth my people the children of Israel out of Egypt.
>
> EXODUS 3:7–10

Reading this history should hearten you, should make you realize that if faith is yours, freedom can be yours, also. Do your part by praying for help:

> Arise, O Lord; O God, lift up thine hand: forget not the humble.
>
> PSALMS 10:12

If you stand alone against those who persecute you, it is true that you are not very powerful, but enlist in the Lord's army, and your strength is suddenly manifold:

> But the Lord is with me as a mighty terrible one:
> therefore my persecutors shall stumble, and they shall
> not prevail: they shall be greatly ashamed; for they shall
> not prosper: their everlasting confusion shall never be
> forgotten.
>
> JEREMIAH 20:11

We all know what it is to experience fear when facing the injustice of persecution. But reading Scripture, and understanding that these words have been inspired by God, can help instill within us a God-given bravery:

> Thus saith thy Lord the Lord, and thy God that plead-
> eth the cause of his people, Behold, I have taken out of
> thine hand the cup of trembling, even the dregs of the
> cup of my fury; thou shalt no more drink it again:
> But I will put it into the hand of them that afflict thee;
> which have said to thy soul, Bow down, that we may go
> over: and thou hast laid thy body as the ground, and
> as the street, to them that went over.
>
> ISAIAH 51:22-23

Remember that the Word of the Lord is infallible, and you can place your trust in Him who has promised:

> The Lord thy God in the midst of thee is mighty; he
> will save, he will rejoice over thee with joy; he will rest
> in his love, he will joy over thee with singing.
> I will gather them that are sorrowful for the solemn
> assembly, who are of thee, to whom the reproach of it
> was a burden.
> Behold, at that time I will undo all that afflict thee:
> and I will save her that halteth, and gather her that was
> driven out; and I will get them praise and fame in every
> land where they have been put to shame.
>
> ZEPHANIAH 3:17-19

No matter how much you may suffer, no matter how heavy the oppressions laid upon you, can you compare

your suffering to those experienced by the Son of God
who went to the cross to save all of us?

> I am crucified with Christ: nevertheless I live; yet not
> I, but Christ liveth in me: and the life which I now live
> in the flesh I live by the faith of the Son of God, who
> loved me, and gave himself for me.
>
> GALATIANS 2:20

Our Saviour died to save us, to give us the liberty of
everlasting life. It is a liberty—a freedom—we must be
thankful for every day. Remember Paul's words:

> Stand fast therefore in the liberty wherewith Christ
> hath made us free, and be not entangled again with the
> yoke of bondage.
>
> GALATIANS 5:1

Remember your own past suffering once you are freed
of the yoke of oppression. Express your own happiness by
being kind and generous to those around you:

> Also thou shalt not oppress a stranger: for ye know the
> heart of a stranger, seeing ye were strangers in the land
> of Egypt.
>
> EXODUS 23:9

Be joyful when you come in to your time of freedom,
and never forget to offer thanks to the Lord of Glory who
makes all things possible to His children who believe in
Him:

> Therefore the redeemed of the Lord shall return, and
> come with singing unto Zion; and everlasting joy shall
> be upon their head: they shall obtain gladness and joy;
> and sorrow and mourning shall flee away.
> I, even I, am he that comforteth you: who art thou,
> that thou shouldest be afraid of a man that shall die, and
> of the son of man which shall be made as grass;

And forgettest the Lord thy maker, that hath stretched forth the heavens, and laid the foundations of the earth; and hast feared continually every day because of the fury of the oppressor, as if he were ready to destroy? And where is the fury of the oppressor?

ISAIAH 51:11–13

We then, as workers together with him, beseech you also that ye receive not the grace of God in vain.

(For he saith, I have heard thee in a time accepted, and in the day of salvation have I succored thee: behold, now is the accepted time; behold, now is the day of salvation.)

II CORINTHIANS 6:1–2

Perhaps you have prayed, and prayed again, but yet you have not achieved the freedom you so long for. Can there ever be too much prayer? The Holy Book of God is so filled with prayers that are meant to comfort you, that you can find solace on almost every page.

God and His Son have always been aware of the many people who have been painfully oppressed through the ages, and the Bible bears witness to their loving care:

Lord, thou hast heard the desire of the humble: thou wilt prepare their heart, thou wilt cause thine ear to hear:

To judge the fatherless and the oppressed, that the man of the earth may no more oppress.

PSALMS 10:17–18

Save me, O God, by thy name, and judge me by thy strength.

Hear my prayer, O God; give ear to the words of my mouth.

For strangers are risen up against me, and oppressors seek after my soul: they have not set God before them. Selah.

Behold, God is mine helper: the Lord is with them that uphold my soul.

He shall reward evil unto mine enemies: cut them off in thy truth.

I will freely sacrifice unto thee: I will praise thy name, O Lord; for it is good.

For he hath delivered me out of all trouble: and mine eyes hath seen his desire upon mine enemies.

PSALMS 54:1–7

Comfort ye, comfort ye my people, saith your God.

ISAIAH 40:1

As a true believer, you know there are many kinds of oppression, the worst being the oppression of the soul and the spirit. But the grace of faith has made you understand that the worst of the oppressions can be removed from you with the help of God and gentle Jesus.

The Bible tells us very plainly that nothing is impossible if it comes from the Holy Spirit:

The wolf also shall dwell with the lamb, and the leopard shall lie down with the kid; and the calf and the young lion and the fatling together; and a little child shall lead them.

And the cow and the bear shall feed; their young ones shall lie down together: and the lion shall eat straw like the ox.

And the sucking child shall play on the hole of the asp, and the weaned child shall put his hand on the cockatrice' den.

They shall not hurt nor destroy in all my holy mountain: for the earth shall be full of the knowledge of the Lord, as the waters cover the sea.

ISAIAH 11:6–9

Isaiah was given his great gift of prophecy by God. When he said that a little child would lead them, of course he was prophesying the coming of the infant Jesus. Hold your hand out to Him, and He will lift the burden of oppression from your soul.

Poverty

There is more than one kind of poverty, and most of us have suffered from its various manifestations at different times in our lives.

There is poverty of the heart, poverty of the mind, poverty of the soul, and poverty of worldly possessions. All poverty is painful to those who suffer the pangs of doing without.

Our Saviour did not want us to be poor in any way. He offered us Himself as the bread of life—the greatest spiritual gift ever given to man—and He also fed the multitudes with loaves and fishes when they hungered for actual food.

When you are assailed by any kind of poverty, look to God's Word; the Bible offers consolation within its pages:

> For the needy shall not always be forgotten: the expectation of the poor shall not perish for ever.
>
> PSALMS 9:18

Remember those words and rid yourself of poverty of the spirit by sharing what you have with others less fortunate. Our Saviour was concerned with physical as well as spiritual hungers:

> And when it was evening, his disciples came to him, saying, This is a desert place, and the time is now past; send the multitude away, that they may go into the villages, and buy themselves victuals.

But Jesus said unto them, They need not depart; give ye them to eat.

And they say unto him, We have here but five loaves, and two fishes.

He said, Bring them hither to me.

And he commanded the multitude to sit down on the grass, and took the five loaves, and the two fishes, and looking up to heaven, he blessed, and brake, and gave the loaves to his disciples, and the disciples to the multitude.

And they did all eat, and were filled: and they took up of the fragments that remained twelve baskets full.

And they that had eaten were about five thousand men, beside women and children.

MATTHEW 14:15–21

Are you poor in heart? Understand that you need not remain so: If you come to your heavenly Father with your prayers, he will heed you, much as any father will try to soothe and comfort his children:

Or what man is there of you, whom if his son ask bread, will he give him a stone?

Or if he ask a fish, will he give him a serpent?

If ye then, being evil, know how to give good gifts unto your children, how much more shall your Father which is in heaven give good things to them that ask him?

MATTHEW 7:9–11

Are you truly poor, or do you yearn to pile abundance upon abundance? If this, in some measure, describes you, learn to be satisfied with what you have when it is truly enough:

A good name is rather to be chosen than great riches, and loving favor rather than silver and gold.

The rich and poor meet together: the Lord is the maker of them all.

PROVERBS 22:1–2

God looks with compassion upon all those who are poor. Pray to Him for help:

> When the poor and needy seek water, and there is none, and their tongue faileth for thirst, I the Lord will hear them, I the God of Israel will not forsake them.
> I will open rivers in high places, and fountains in the midst of the valleys: I will make the wilderness a pool of water, and the dry land springs of water.
>
> ISAIAH 41:17–18

At this moment you may be poor, but God will open the hearts of those who have more than you, and His words will make them understand your plight and stretch out their hands to you. Remember to do the same for your fellows should you become more fortunate:

> He that oppresseth the poor reproacheth his Maker: but he that honoreth him hath mercy on the poor.
>
> PROVERBS 14:31

Our beloved Saviour had special compassion on those who were poor in possessions. Remember His promise:

> And he lifted up his eyes on his disciples, and said, Blessed be ye poor: for yours is the kingdom of God.
> Blessed are ye that hunger now: for ye shall be filled. Blessed are ye that weep now: for ye shall laugh.
> Blessed are ye, when men shall hate you, and when they shall separate you from their company, and shall reproach you, and cast out your name as evil, for the Son of man's sake.
> Rejoice ye in that day, and leap for joy: for, behold, your reward is great in heaven: for in the like manner did their fathers unto the prophets.
>
> LUKE 6:20–23

The Son of God was truly troubled by those who had much and would not share their wealth. It was better to be poor than to lack generosity:

But woe unto you that are rich! for ye have received your consolation.

Woe unto you that are full! for ye shall hunger. Woe unto you that laugh now! for ye shall mourn and weep.

LUKE 6:24–25

To rid yourself of the worst kind of poverty—poverty of the soul—cultivate the giving spirit. Give of yourself to others, and come openly to Jesus Christ, offering Him yourself completely for your salvation's sake:

And Jesus sat over against the treasury, and beheld how people cast money into the treasury: and many that were rich cast in much.

And there came a certain poor widow, and she threw in two mites, which make a farthing.

And he called unto him his disciples, and saith unto them, Verily I say unto you, That this poor widow hath cast more in, than all they which have cast into the treasury:

For all they did cast in of their abundance; but she of her want did cast in all that she had, even all her living.

MARK 12:41–44

You will never feel spiritually poor again if you accept the great gift of life everlasting being offered to you by Jesus Christ:

They shall hunger no more, neither thirst any more; neither shall the sun light on them, nor any heat.

For the Lamb which is in the midst of the throne shall feed them, and shall lead them unto living fountains of waters: and God shall wipe away all tears from their eyes.

REVELATION 7:16–17

What is the greatest wealth of all? The wealth acquired by the soul which comes to God with love and in humility, and is loved and forgiven in turn:

> Ho, every one that thirsteth, come ye to the waters, and he that hath no money; come ye, buy, and eat; yea, come, buy wine and milk without money and without price.
>
> Wherefore do ye spend money for that which is not bread? And your labor for that which satisfieth not? Harken diligently unto me, and eat ye that which is good, and let your soul delight itself in fatness.
>
> ISAIAH 55:1–2

Our Heavenly Father judges His children equally, and He does not look with special favor upon those who may have acquired great wealth. Therefore, in the eyes of God, you are rich because you are worthy of salvation:

> Let all those that seek thee rejoice and be glad in thee: let such as love thy salvation say continually, The Lord be magnified.
>
> But I am poor and needy; yet the Lord thinketh upon me: thou art my help and my deliverer; make no tarrying, O my God.
>
> PSALMS 40:16–17

As God has special compassion for the poor, so He has special love for those who care about their poorer brothers:

> Blessed is he that considereth the poor: the Lord will deliver him in time of trouble.
>
> The Lord will preserve him, and keep him alive; and he shall be blessed upon the earth: and thou wilt not deliver him unto the will of his enemies.
>
> PSALMS 41:1–2

But those who do not feel sympathy for others cannot expect sympathy from Him on high:

> Whoso stoppeth his ears at the cry of the poor, he also shall cry himself, but shall not be heard.
>
> PROVERBS 21:13

The Bible tells us that though we may own little, if we can share it with a loving and happy family, we are truly wealthy:

> Better is a dry morsel, and quietness therewith, than a house full of sacrifices with strife.
>
> PROVERBS 17:1

Put your trust in God, and go for comfort to Jesus Christ. He who loves you will help satisfy your wants, and as you love Him, remember that He asked you this prayer:

> After this manner therefore pray ye: Our Father which art in heaven, Hallowed be thy name.
> Thy kingdom come. Thy will be done in earth, as it is in heaven.
> Give us this day our daily bread.
>
> MATTHEW 6:9–11

Let peace come to you, your pleas will not be denied if you have faith in the Son of God, because He has told us:

> And I say unto you, Ask, and it shall be given you; seek, and ye shall find; knock, and it shall be opened unto you.
> For every one that asketh receiveth; and he that seeketh findeth; and to him that knocketh it shall be opened.
>
> LUKE 11:9–11

Prejudice and Intolerance

The Bible tells us, over and over again, that we are to love one another. That was the message brought to us by the beloved Son of God, Jesus Christ. However, as in many other things, it is not always easy to do His Will.

Everyone is harmed by prejudice and by intolerance. The idea that some people are not as good as others because they are different divides people, keeps them apart, and stops them from loving one another. The message of the Holy Scriptures is that we should love each other, just as we hope to be loved by our Saviour.

Who is hurt most? The one who says, "You are not as good as I am, therefore I cannot like you," or the one who hears those words said to him? Everyone is damaged by such feelings. The person who holds a prejudice does not let love take root in his heart, and the one who is hurt by the prejudice is likely to react with hate, and eventually, with prejudices of his own.

Our Saviour has told us that God's most important commandments are:

> And thou shalt love the Lord thy God with all thy heart, and with all thy soul, and with all thy mind, and with all thy strength: this is the first commandment.
> And the second is like, namely this, Thou shalt love thy neighbor as thyself. There is none other commandment greater than these.
>
> MARK 12:30–31

Sometimes, people hold prejudices secretly in their hearts; they don't want to admit to them; perhaps they are even a little ashamed of these feelings. However, if a person is prejudiced, he inevitably will act out of his dislike of another person or a group of people. His intolerant attitudes will burst forth; it will be evident to all that his heart is held in a cold vise, and that his days are filled with darkness rather than with the light of Christ's love:

> He that saith he is in the light, and hateth his brother, is in darkness even until now.
> He that loveth his brother abideth in the light, and there is none occasion of stumbling in him.
> But he that hateth his brother is in darkness, and walketh in darkness, and knoweth not whither he goeth, because that darkness hath blinded his eyes.
>
> I JOHN 2:9–11

You may know what it is to be the victim of prejudice, and you can be a victim whether you have hurt someone else by your intolerance, or you have been hurt by another's intolerance of you. Whichever the case, pray that the light of understanding will reach all hearts. It is important to feel the intensity of these words:

> But before faith came, we were kept under the law, shut up unto the faith which should afterwards be revealed.
> Wherefore the law was our schoolmaster to bring us unto Christ, that we might be justified by faith.
> But after that faith is come, we are no longer under a schoolmaster.
> For ye are all the children of God by faith in Christ Jesus.
> For as many of you as have been baptized into Christ have put on Christ.
> There is neither Jew nor Greek, there is neither bond nor free, there is neither male nor female: for ye are all one in Christ Jesus.
>
> GALATIANS 3:23–28

Even at this moment, you, or someone you know, may be thinking, But how can I love this other person? How can I even like him? He is so very different from me. We have nothing in common. These thoughts go against God's Word, which makes it very clear we are all one family:

> Have we not all one father? Hath not one God created us? Why do we deal treacherously every man against his brother, by profaning the covenant of our fathers?
>
> MALACHI 2:10

Prejudice is painful to our Lord, Jesus Christ. He came to redeem us, and He loves us all, just as God showed His love for us by sending us His Son. Anyone who recognizes this great love and benevolence must understand that to discriminate against others is to deny God's love.

If you honestly feel that you are open to receive the love of Jesus, then open your heart and your mind. Let the warmth of our Saviour's love flow through you, so that in time you can extend your hand and your love to others:

> Whosoever hateth his brother is a murderer: and ye know that no murderer hath eternal life abiding in him.
>
> Hereby perceive we the love of God, because he laid down his life for us: and we ought to lay down our lives for the brethren.
>
> But whoso hath this world's good, and seeth his brother have need, and shutteth up his bowels of compassion from him, how dwelleth the love of God in him?
>
> My little children, let us not love in word, neither in tongue; but in deed and in truth.
>
> And hereby we know that we are of the truth, and shall assure our hearts before him.
>
> I JOHN 3:15–19

Often, prejudice stems from ignorance, or from lack of knowledge. This other person—these other people—they are different from you and me? What are they really like?

They are strange, their customs are different, their habits are not the same as ours, how can we trust them? But the Scriptures tell us that these very differences may be important to us:

> Let brotherly love continue.
> Be not forgetful to entertain strangers: for thereby some have entertained angels unawares.
>
> HEBREWS 13:1–2

Think of your closest friend: weren't you strangers to each other at one time? Have you ever moved to a new city or community? You were the stranger then. Remember how happy you were when new neighbors reached out their hands to you. The Bible tells us to do the same for others in memory of the time when we, too, wandered in a strange land:

> Thou shalt neither vex a stranger, nor oppress him: for ye were strangers in the land of Egypt.
>
> EXODUS 22:21

If you still find it hard to uproot the prejudice in your heart, or you know that others cannot seem to rid themselves of their prejudice against you, remind yourself that we were told:

> Wherefore receive ye one another, as Christ also received us to the glory of God.
>
> ROMANS 15:7

Often, intolerance stems from the insistence that we are qualified to judge others. We *judge* that the differences between people are bad; we *judge* that the way others do things is wrong. We judge, and judge, and keep on judging, when the Scriptures tell us over and over again that making judgments about other people is not within our province:

But why dost thou judge thy brother? Or why dost thou set at nought thy brother? For we shall all stand before the judgment seat of Christ.

For it is written, As I live, saith the Lord, every knee shall bow to me, and every tongue shall confess to God.

So then every one of us shall give account of himself to God.

Let us not therefore judge one another any more: but judge this rather, that no man put a stumblingblock or an occasion to fail in his brother's way.

ROMANS 14:10–13

If you know in your heart that you are prone to make judgments about other people, ask yourself how you would feel if they were to judge you:

Judge not, and ye shall not be judged: condemn not, and ye shall not be condemned: forgive, and ye shall be forgiven:

Give, and it shall be given unto you; good measure, pressed down, and shaken together, and running over, shall men give unto your bosom. For with the same measure that ye mete withal it shall be measured to you again.

LUKE 6:37–38

Why does our Saviour plead with us so strenuously not to judge others? Because if we come to Jesus Christ with a true and humble spirit, we realize that only He and His Father are capable of judgment.

We are not wise enough, or clear-sighted enough to inflict our opinion upon others, nor are we ever so completely free of blame that we have the right to impose judgment:

And why beholdest thou the mote that is in thy brother's eye, but perceiveth not the beam that is in thine own eye?

Either how canst thou say to thy brother, Brother, let me pull out the mote that is in thine eye, when thou thyself beholdest not the beam that is in thine own eye? Thou hypocrite, cast out first the beam out of thine own eye, and then shalt thou see clearly to pull out the mote that is in thy brother's eye.

LUKE 6:41–42

Many people say, "Very well, for our Saviour's sake, I will tolerate these other people." But toleration is not enough. Our Lord talks about love, and about helping others as they travel through the rocky paths of life, and about giving with an open heart to everyone:

Bear ye one another's burdens, and so fulfil the law of Christ.

GALATIANS 6:2

And above all things have fervent charity among yourselves: for charity shall cover the multitude of sins.
Use hospitality one to another without grudging.

I PETER 4:8–9

How can prejudice be uprooted from the mind, intolerance from the heart? So often these feelings are based on terrible lessons taught to us, and to others, when we were children.

Shall we, now, go against things that we were told were "absolutely gospel"? Yes, we must do just that, because often people use the word "gospel" too lightly, *The Gospel* is God's Word, it is contained within His inspired Scriptures, and it is the *only Gospel* that we pay heed to:

Thou shalt not hate thy brother in thine heart: thou shalt in any wise rebuke thy neighbor, and not suffer sin upon him.

LEVITICUS 19:17

But I say unto you, That whosoever is angry with his
brother without a cause shall be in danger of the judgment: and whosoever shall say to his brother, Raca, shall
be in danger of the council: but whosoever shall say,
Thou fool, shall be in danger of hell fire.

MATTHEW 5:22

One way to aid those suffering from prejudice is to remind them—and ourselves—that all true believers will
spend eternity with Him who died for us on the cross. We
are all His children. If we look forward to this eternity
spent with our brothers, we should try to be close to them
here on earth:

The Spirit itself beareth witness with our spirit, that
we are the children of God:
And if children, then heirs; heirs of God, and joint-
heirs with Christ; if so be that we suffer with him, that
we may be also glorified together.

ROMANS 8:16–17

Being prejudiced against others, behaving intolerantly,
does nothing good for the people who harbor these feelings. Indeed, where they might enjoy the love of Christ
and their fellowmen, they experience, instead, a sense of
desolation. They do not know why they feel this heavy
sadness, but yet it is with them. It is the same desolation
visited by God upon those who would not hear Him when
He asked all to show compassion to their brothers:

Thus speaketh the Lord of hosts, saying, Execute true
judgment, and show mercy and compassions every man
to his brother:
And oppress not the widow, nor the fatherless, the
stranger, nor the poor; and let none of you imagine evil
against his brother in your heart.
But they refused to hearken, and pulled away the

shoulder, and stopped their ears, that they should not hear.

Yea, they made their hearts as an adamant stone, lest they should hear the law, and the words which the Lord of hosts hath sent in his spirit by the former prophets: therefore came a great wrath from the Lord of hosts.

Therefore it is come to pass, that as he cried, and they would not hear; so they cried, and I would not hear, saith the Lord of hosts:

But I scattered them with a whirlwind among all the nations whom they knew not. Thus the land was desolate after them, that no man passed through nor returned: for they laid the pleasant land desolate.

ZECHARIAH 7:9–14

Being prejudiced cuts us off from others whom we might grow to love given the chance. It also goes against the words of the Holy Scriptures:

Therefore all things whatsoever ye would that men should do to you, do ye even so to them: for this is the law and the prophets.

MATTHEW 7:12

Remember the message repeated over and over again in God's Book: we should love one another; we should be as kind to others as we would have them be to us. This is God's law, and the law of His Son who has said:

Jesus answered and said unto him, if a man love me, he will keep my words: and my Father will love him, and we will come unto him, and make our abode with him.

JOHN 14:23

The heavy burdens carried by the prejudiced heart can be lightened by the love of Jesus.

Rejection

What does rejection mean to you? You may have been rejected in ways that range from minor to serious: perhaps
you've been refused admittance when applying to a special
school, or you may have been denied a particular job. You
may have known rejection when you've applied for a loan,
or tried to rent an apartment.

All rejection hurts, and all of us have experienced one
or more kinds of rejection. However, a most painful rejection is the one we experience when someone we love
does not reciprocate that love.

This kind of rejection can be particularly shattering.
We start reexamining ourselves; we wonder about our
intrinsic value and worth. We stop seeing ourselves as we
really are, and begin to regard ourselves as we are mir-
rored in someone else's eyes. Something is wrong with us,
that is evident. But what is it? How can the person to
whom we offered our love find us so unworthy to be loved
in return?

It is only natural to go through this kind of self-reevalu-
ation, yet even as we do so, it is important to remember
that He who was the worthiest of love was rejected by
many. And no matter how many people may reject us,
God the Father and His Son still find us worthy of Their
love:

> The stone which the builders refused is become the
> head stone of the corner.

This is the Lord's doing; it is marvelous in our eyes.

This is the day which the Lord hath made; we will rejoice and be glad in it.

Save now, I beseech thee, O Lord: O Lord, I beseech thee, send now prosperity.

PSALMS 118:22-25

Perhaps as you are suffering the smart of painful rejection, you are thinking that you will never care for anyone ever again. You plan to live out your days, tightly closed within yourself, hoping to avoid the possibility of future pain. But if you do this, you are rejecting yourself! Only by being an open person can you hope that another person will hold out his hand to you. Be generous —not just with what you own—but with yourself:

Cast thy bread upon the waters: for thou shalt find it after many days.

Give a portion to seven, and also to eight; for thou knowest not what evil shall be upon the earth.

ECCLESIASTES 11:1-2

Instead of dwelling on your rejection, go to the Word of God for comfort:

Blessed be God, even the Father of our Lord Jesus Christ, the Father of mercies, and the God of all comfort;

Who comforteth us in all our tribulation, that we may be able to comfort them which are in any trouble, by the comfort wherewith we ourselves are comforted of God.

II CORINTHIANS 1:3-4

The most soul-shattering rejection any of us can experience is when we are rejected *because* of our faith in our Lord, Jesus Christ.

We may be able to understand that people can turn

from us, but how can they turn from the Saviour? But, yet, He told us that this very thing would happen:

> If ye were of the world, the world would love his own; but because ye are not of the world, but I have chosen you out of the world, therefore the world hateth you.
>
> Remember the word that I said unto you, The servant is not greater than his lord. If they have persecuted me, they will also persecute you; if they have kept my saying, they will keep yours also.
>
> But all these things will they do unto you for my name's sake, because they know not him that sent me.
>
> If I had not come and spoken unto them, they had not had sin; but now they have no cloak for their sin.
>
> He that hateth me hateth my Father also.
>
> If I had not done among them the works which none other man did, they had not had sin: but now have they both seen and hated both me and my Father.
>
> But this cometh to pass, that the word might be fulfilled that is written in their law, They hated me with a cause.
>
> JOHN 15:19–25

Can you possibly cope with this rejection? Are you strong enough? You can be! Throw your shoulders back, march forward, remembering that you are in the army of our Lord:

> Thou therefore, my son, be strong in the grace that is in Christ Jesus.
>
> And the things that thou hast heard of me among many witnesses, the same commit thou to faithful men, who shall be able to teach others also.
>
> Thou therefore endure hardness, as a good soldier of Jesus Christ.
>
> II TIMOTHY 2:1–3

> Beareth all things, believeth all things, hopeth all things, endureth all things.
>
> I CORINTHIANS 13:7

What can you do to those who reject you and reject our Saviour? Should you reach out with a fist, try in some way to harm them as you believe they have harmed you? We have been advised to do just the opposite—the Word of God tells us that we must behave in a charitable, kindly manner to all:

> Though I speak with the tongues of men and of angels, and have not charity, I am become as sounding brass, or a tinkling cymbal.
>
> I CORINTHIANS 13:1

We know that the Son of God accepted rejection for our sakes. Now, it is our turn to persevere when we are rejected for His sake:

> He that heareth you heareth me; he that despiseth you despiseth me; and he that despiseth me despiseth him that sent me.
>
> LUKE 10:16

> Blessed are ye, when men shall revile you, and persecute you, and shall say all manner of evil against you falsely, for my sake.
>
> MATTHEW 5:11

What do we finally come to understand as we are rebuffed by those who also rebuff our Lord? As they reject us, He accepts us and loves us. It is not other people who matter, it is the loving kindness of God and our Saviour that we yearn for:

> But seek ye first the kingdom of God, and his righteousness; and all these things shall be added unto you.
> Take therefore no thought for the morrow: for the morrow shall take thought for the things of itself. Sufficient unto the day is the evil thereof.
>
> MATTHEW 6:33-34

The next time you are turned away, remember that it is acceptance and entrance to our Father's house that you wish to gain. And you will not be forgotten, if you suffer rejection for His Son's sake:

> When the Son of man shall come in his glory, and all the holy angels with him, then shall he sit upon the throne of his glory:
>
> And before him shall be gathered all nations: and he shall separate them one from another, as a shepherd divideth his sheep from the goats:
>
> And he shall set the sheep on his right hand, but the goats on the left.
>
> Then shall the King say unto them on his right hand, Come, ye blessed of my Father, inherit the kingdom prepared for you from the foundation of the world:
>
> For I was ahungered, and ye gave me meat: I was thirsty, and ye gave me drink: I was a stranger, and ye took me in:
>
> Naked, and ye clothed me: I was sick, and ye visited me: I was in prison and ye came unto me.
>
> MATTHEW 25:31–36

> For many are called, but few are chosen.
>
> MATTHEW 22:14

Repentance

Just as we are all capable of sinning, so we are all capable of repenting. Indeed, if we do not repent, we remain in the state where we are far from God's love.

Being unloved by family, friends, people whom we love is a lonely state. Being unloved by God is to be lonely and lost forever.

It is because we want to come close to God that we understand the need for repentance. Just as when we were children we came to our parents to say, "Sorry," so, now, we want to come to our Heavenly Father and say the same thing.

Because we are God's beloved children, He has given us the way in which we may draw near to Him once again. He placed His beloved Son here on earth, and allowed our Saviour to offer Himself as a sacrifice for all our sins.

We are saved when we fully believe in Christ's sacrifice for us and accept that sacrifice. We understand that even though we are guilty, we can be forgiven when we go to Jesus, and ask Him to take us by the hand, leading us back to our Father.

If you are heavy in heart, and you want to come penitently to Jesus Christ, the Holy Scriptures can show you the way. God's Word tells us we will not have to face His Judgment if we repent, and accept our redemption through the sacrifice of His Son:

> Verily, verily, I say unto you, He that heareth my
> word, and believeth on him that sent me, hath everlast-

ing life, and shall not come into condemnation; but is passed from death unto life.

JOHN 5:24

You may be in trouble, and done some things that you are truly ashamed of. Perhaps you feel overwhelmed by the depravity of your deeds, and you are afraid that God will destroy you, but the Bible tells us this is not so:

> When thou art in tribulation, and all these things are come upon thee, even in the latter days, if thou turn to the Lord thy God, and shalt be obedient unto his voice;
> (For the Lord thy God is a merciful God;) he will not forsake thee, neither destroy thee, nor forget the covenant of thy fathers which he sware unto them.
>
> DEUTERONOMY 4:30–31

Isaiah prophesied how God would show us His great mercy and let all of us who are contrite come once again to Him through His beloved Son:

> For a small moment have I forsaken thee; but with great mercies will I gather thee.
> In a little wrath I hid my face from thee for a moment; but with everlasting kindness will I have mercy on thee, saith the Lord thy Redeemer.
>
> ISAIAH 54:7–8

God's love is truly marvelous, and as we long for it, and accept it happily, we must also learn to accept those times when He reproves us:

> My son, despise not the chastening of the Lord; neither be weary of his correction:
> For whom the Lord loveth he correcteth; even as a father the son in whom he delighteth.
>
> PROVERBS 3:11–12

Can you doubt that you are one of the children in whom God delights? It is not possible to do so when we remember that God sacrificed His Son, so that we can come penitently through that sacrifice to His side. The Word of God speaks of many sacrifices that have been made in the past, but it was our Saviour who made the ultimate sacrifice for us:

> Neither by the blood of goats and calves, but by his own blood he entered in once into the holy place, having obtained eternal redemption for us.
>
> HEBREWS 9:12

Not a day passes but that we remember what He did for us. And He expects so little in return—only that we offer Him true repentance:

> Repent ye therefore, and be converted, that your sins may be blotted out, when the times of refreshing shall come from the presence of the Lord;
> And he shall send Jesus Christ, which before was preached unto you:
> Whom the heaven must receive until the times of restitution of all things, which God hath spoken by the mouth of all his holy prophets since the world began.
>
> ACTS 3:19-21

The Holy Scriptures tell us that the truly penitent who turn to Jesus will be saved. Saved, and happy once again:

> Therefore with joy shall ye draw water out of the wells of salvation.
> And in that day shall ye say, Praise the Lord, call upon his name, declare his doings among the people, make mention that his name is exalted.
> Sing unto the Lord; for he hath done excellent things: this is known in all the earth.
>
> ISAIAH 12:3-5

The Bible reminds us of these true facts: it is not enough to merely say, "I'm sorry," and then try to atone for past misdeeds. To obtain forgiveness, we must approach our Father through His Son:

> Not by works of righteousness which we have done, but according to his mercy he saved us, by the washing of regeneration, and renewing of the Holy Ghost;
> Which he shed on us abundantly through Jesus Christ our Saviour.
>
> TITUS 3:5–6

Can you say, "I am truly sorry for my sins, I am regretful, I will try not to sin again"? Sometimes it is hard to admit that we are wrong. If this is one of your problems, look to the Book, and see how others have humbled themselves before God:

> Wherefore I abhor myself, and repent in dust and ashes.
>
> JOB 42:6

> Therefore also now, saith the Lord, turn ye even to me with all your heart, and with fasting, and with weeping and with mourning:
> And rend your heart, and not your garments, and turn unto the Lord your God: for he is gracious and merciful, slow to anger, and of great kindness, and repenteth him of the evil.
>
> JOEL 2:12–13

Why does the Word of God advise us to rend our hearts and not our clothes? Because if we want to be forgiven, we must be *truly* sorry—sorry to the depths of our souls, and not merely pretending to regret past sins.

God will forgive us for His Son's sake if we approach Him openly and honestly, as little children approach an earthly father:

> I write unto you, little children, because your sins are forgiven you for his name's sake.
>
> I JOHN 2:12

There may come days when you consider yourself so sinful that you fear that you will never be forgiven. You see people around you who always seem to do the right thing. How lucky they are! Unlike you, they have nothing to be sorry about. Read what the Bible has to say about that, and you will be much comforted:

> I say unto you, that likewise joy shall be in heaven over one sinner that repenteth, more than over ninety and nine just persons, which need no repentance.
>
> LUKE 15:7

Understand, too, that there is no one who is not in need of forgiveness:

> For all have sinned, and come short of the glory of God.
>
> ROMANS 3:23

The person who claims he has never done anything wrong is probably the most sinful person of all, because he has never come to realize the need for repentance:

> If we say that we have no sin, we deceive ourselves, and the truth is not in us.
> If we confess our sins, he is faithful and just to forgive us our sins, and to cleanse us from all unrighteousness.
>
> I JOHN 1:8–9

There is a great deal of difference in being a righteous person and in being a self-righteous man who is so smug that he can never admit to any faults. The Word of God counsels us:

> Confess your faults one to another, and pray one for another, that ye may be healed. The effectual fervent prayer of a righteous man availeth much.
>
> JAMES 5:16

A truly repentant person knows that he can turn humbly to God:

> Therefore turn thou to thy God: keep mercy and judgment and wait on thy God continually.
>
> HOSEA 12:6

> Cast thy burden upon the Lord, and he shall sustain thee: he shall never suffer the righteous to be moved.
>
> PSALMS 55:22

Perhaps, in past times, you have been truly sorry—truly penitent. You have come to Jesus and felt cleansed, but then you have gone on to do things you regret.

Once again, you repent, but you fear that our Saviour will not accept you, and your faith wavers. Understand that He loves you, and though He is sorrowful about you, you can always come to Him and be healed:

> And when the scribes and Pharisees saw him eat with publicans and sinners, they said unto his disciples, How is it that he eateth and drinketh with publicans and sinners?
>
> When Jesus heard it, he saith unto them, They that are whole have no need of the physician, but they that are sick: I came not to call the righteous, but sinners to repentance.
>
> MARK 2:16–17

If there are times when you feel that your soul is so troubled that you are beyond even His help, remember those who have cried out in spiritual pain, and say with them:

> Unto thee lift I up mine eyes, O thou that dwellest in the heavens.
>
> Behold, as the eyes of servants look unto the hand of their masters, and as the eyes of a maiden unto the hand

of her mistress; so our eyes wait upon the Lord our God, until that he have mercy upon us.

Have mercy upon us, O Lord, have mercy upon us: for we are exceedingly filled with contempt.

Our soul is exceedingly filled with the scorning of those that are at ease, and with the contempt of the proud.

PSALMS 123:1–4

You are not the only person to feel shameful about some of your acts, and regretful about those days when you have not lived close to Jesus:

Wherefore came I forth out of the womb to see labor and sorrow, that my days should be consumed with shame?

JEREMIAH 20:18

But what do the Holy Scriptures advise us when we feel this way? They tell us that there is always another chance given to those who repent:

Let the wicked forsake his way, and the unrighteous man his thoughts: and let him return unto the Lord, and he will have mercy upon him; and to our God, for he will abundantly pardon.

ISAIAH 55:7

If you are floundering in a state of guilt, you can be relieved of this terrible pressure and return to God when you remember that His Son was put on earth for the express purpose of saving all those who are penitent and will accept Him as the Redeemer.

Him hath God exalted with his right hand to be a Prince and a Saviour, for to give repentance to Israel, and forgiveness of sins.

ACTS 5:31

The Bible tells us that if we truly repent, we will not only be forgiven our sins, but we will also come to a life eternal with our Saviour:

> But he, whom God raised again, saw no corruption.
> Be it known unto you therefore, men and brethren, that through this man is preached unto you the forgiveness of sins.
>
> ACTS 13:37–38

A loving God has given us His Son and the Holy Ghost to intercede for us when we truly repent:

> Then said Jesus to them again, Peace be unto you: as my Father hath sent me, even so send I you.
> And when he had said this, he breathed on them, and saith unto them, Receive ye the Holy Ghost:
> Whose soever sins ye remit, they are remitted unto them; and whose soever sins ye retain, they are retained.
>
> JOHN 20:21–23

The Bible repeats one lesson many times over: as we welcome the forgiveness of our Lord Jesus Christ, so we should be able to offer our small forgiveness when others tell us that they are sorry:

> And be ye kind one to another, tender-hearted, forgiving one another, even as God for Christ's sake hath forgiven you.
>
> EPHESIANS 4:32

We have admitted our guilt, we have come to our Redeemer for salvation, and we now walk happily in His light:

> For ye were sometimes darkness, but now are ye light in the Lord: walk as children of light.
>
> EPHESIANS 5:8

The soul who experiences the cleansing power of the Saviour is a joyful soul. This is the time to offer thanks to God for the great gift that He has given us:

> O praise the Lord, all ye nations: praise him, all ye people.
> For his merciful kindness is great toward us: and the truth of the Lord endureth for ever. Praise ye the Lord.
>
> PSALMS 117:1–2

In the future, God's Word asks us to remember that His goodness, and our Saviour's forgiveness, are always with us.

In return for all the loving kindness shown to us, we are instructed to act with love, mercy, and justice, and to carry humbleness in our hearts:

> Wherewith shall I come before the Lord, and bow my-self before the high God? Shall I come before him with burnt offerings, with calves of a year old?
> Will the Lord be pleased with thousands of rams, or with ten thousands of rivers of oil? shall I give my first-born for my transgression, the fruit of my body for the sin of my soul?
> He hath showed thee, O man, what is good; and what doth the Lord require of thee, but to do justly, and to love mercy, and to walk humbly with thy God?
>
> MICAH 6:6–8

Revenge

Have you ever thought, I'm going to get even! Just wait until the next time. All of us, at one time or another, have entertained personal thoughts of revenge.

Frequently, we plot and plan, have fantasies, imaginary conversations wherein we best our enemies, put down those who have done us harm.

Planning to avenge ourselves for slights or cruelties that others have imposed upon us is a natural thought—a human feeling—and failing. And it is a failing, because the greater becomes our concentration on vengeance the less time or heart we have to give our help, our warmth, and our love to others.

Oh, yes, but some people say that revenge—the feeling that we have turned the tables on someone we dislike—is sweet. Sweet enough, so that we are willing to take the consequences of our own bitter actions.

But just how sweet is revenge? According to the poet John Milton:

> Revenge, at first though sweet,
> Bitter ere long back on itself recoils.

Revenge, when finally analyzing the act, does more to hurt the person who exacts it than the person who suffers because of it.

It is because our Creator wanted us to keep whole and healthy, both mentally and spiritually, that He constantly adjured us to leave vengeance to Him. God's Word tells us:

For we know him that hath said, Vengeance belongeth unto me, I will recompense, saith the Lord. And again, The Lord shall judge his people.

HEBREWS 10:30

How do you feel within yourself when the desire for revenge takes over your entire being? Many people, describing their physical reactions when they are concentrating all their efforts on revenge, have said that their stomach muscles tighten, they often have severe headaches, and their hands clench and unclench involuntarily.

This is a terrible way to feel, and it can cause ulcers, migraine headaches, severe back pains, and even heart conditions. It is for this reason that we would do well to heed the advice given to us in the Holy Scriptures:

> Finally, be ye all of one mind, having compassion one of another, love as brethren, be pitiful, be courteous:
>
> Not rendering evil for evil, or railing for railing: but contrariwise blessing; knowing that ye are thereunto called, that ye should inherit a blessing.
>
> For he that will love life, and see good days, let him refrain his tongue from evil, and his lips that they speak no guile:
>
> Let him eschew evil, and do good; let him seek peace, and ensue it.
>
> For the eyes of the Lord are over the righteous, and his ears are open unto their prayers: but the face of the Lord is against them that do evil.
>
> And who is he that will harm you, if ye be followers of that which is good?
>
> But and if ye suffer for righteousness' sake, happy are ye: and be not afraid of their terror, neither be troubled;
>
> But sanctify the Lord God in your hearts: and be ready always to give an answer to every man that asketh you a reason of the hope that is in you, with meekness and fear:
>
> Having a good conscience; that, whereas they speak evil of you, as of evildoers, they may be ashamed that falsely accuse your good conversation in Christ.

> For it is better, if the will of God be so, that ye suffer
> for well doing, than for evil doing.
>
> I PETER 3:8–17

This advice is not easy to follow. Sometimes we feel it
is too great a sacrifice to be asked to give up our desire
for reprisal.

Of course it is a sacrifice! But it is a sacrifice that is not
only good for us, but also healthy for the brotherhood of
Christ, of which we are all members:

> I beseech you therefore, brethren, by the mercies of
> God, that ye present your bodies a living sacrifice, holy,
> acceptable unto God, which is your reasonable service.
>
> And be not conformed to this world: but be ye trans-
> formed by the renewing of your mind, that ye may prove
> what is that good, and acceptable, and perfect, will of
> God.
>
> For I say, through the grace given unto me, to every
> man that is among you, not to think of himself more
> highly than he ought to think; but to think soberly, ac-
> cording as God hath dealt to every man the measure of
> faith.
>
> For as we have many members in one body, and all
> members have not the same office:
>
> So we, being many, are one body in Christ, and every
> one members one of another.
>
> ROMANS 12:1–5

God's Word tells us that we are all one family. That
person who wronged you, and whom you wish to wrong
in return, is not a stranger, but a member of your family
in Christ. We are all His children, and we should leave
chastisement to our Heavenly Father:

> Say not thou, I will recompense evil; but wait on the
> Lord, and he shall save thee.
>
> PROVERBS 20:22

For the Lord is our judge, the Lord is our lawgiver, the Lord is our king; he will save us.

ISAIAH 33:22

But is it possible to be silent, to be patient, to give ourselves over to God, and let Him be the Great Architect of our lives? It is not always possible to do the right things, but it becomes easier to put thoughts of revenge from us when we turn to His Holy Word, and read how, in time, all good things come from Him.

We prayerfully thank Him for not letting us be consumed by our own terrible passion of vindictiveness:

> It is of the Lord's mercies that we are not consumed, because his compassions fail not.
> They are new every morning: great is faithfulness.
> The Lord is my portion, saith my soul; therefore will I hope in him.
> The Lord is good unto them that wait for him, to the soul that seeketh him.
> It is good that a man should both hope and quietly wait for the salvation of the Lord.
> It is good for a man that he bear the yoke in his youth.
> He sitteth alone and keepeth silence, because he hath borne it upon him.
> He putteth his mouth in the dust; if so be there may be hope.
> He giveth his cheek to him that smiteth him: he is filled full with reproach.
> For the Lord will not cast off for ever:
> But though he cause grief, yet will he have compassion according to the multitude of his mercies.

LAMENTATIONS 3:22–32

Perhaps you are arguing that you have been badly hurt, this is the reason for your wish for revenge. But as the Bible tells us not to take weapons of revenge into our own hands, it also tells us that everything that happens to us is according to God's Plan. Was not even His beloved Son hurt? As we remember His pain, our own seems very slight:

> Though he were a Son, yet learned he obedience by the things which he suffered;
> And being made perfect, he became the author of eternal salvation unto all them that obey him.
>
> HEBREWS 5:8–9

Whenever the need to avenge yourself looms larger than any other thought in your mind, read the following over and over, to arrive at a calmer soul:

> Say not, I will do so to him as he hath done to me: I will render to the man according to his work.
>
> PROVERBS 24:29

Always keep in your mind our Saviour's advice on how we should treat our enemies:

> . . . Love your enemies, do good to them which hate you,
> Bless them that curse you, and pray for them which despitefully use you.
> And unto him that smiteth thee on the one cheek offer also the other; and him that taketh away thy cloak forbid not to take thy coat also.
> Give to every man that asketh of thee; and of him that taketh away thy goods ask them not again.
>
> LUKE 6:27–30

As you read those words, you may ponder our Saviour's meaning. How can you possibly be expected to treat an enemy so kindly? As you think about it a bit more, the words take on the light of wisdom. Jesus wanted all of us to love one another, that is His message. And how can you rid yourself of an enemy? Why, by turning him into a friend! And once he is a friend, all desire for revenge disappears.

Of course, it is hard to love an enemy. But this is what our Shepherd wants us to do. He wants us to take the hard road; He wants us to love those who, as yet, do not love us. Because if we take that first step toward loving our enemies, they may take the second step and learn to love us in turn:

> For if ye love them which love you, what thank have ye? For sinners also love those that love them.
> And if ye do good to them which do good to you, what thank have ye? For sinners also do even the same.
>
> LUKE 6:32–33

We must respect the infinite wisdom of our Creator and His Son, who tell us that the weapons of vengeance and judgment do not belong in our hands. If you refuse to heed this advice, and go vengefully your own way, are you ready to accept His judgment?

> Grudge not one against another, brethren, lest ye be condemned: behold, the judge standeth before the door.
>
> JAMES 5:9

The Holy Book tells us again and again that the way of our Saviour is the way of love. If you think "love" each time you want to think "revenge," you will be a happier person, because you will be following His way:

> I therefore, the prisoner of the Lord, beseech you that ye walk worthy of the vocation wherewith ye are called.
> With all lowliness and meekness, with long-suffering, forbearing one another in love;
> Endeavoring to keep the unity of the Spirit in the bond of peace.
>
> EPHESIANS 4:1–3

God's Holy Word contains many requests, beseeching us all to have charity. When this word is used in the Scriptures, it means a great deal more than the giving of money or other worldly goods.

Charity, as it is used in the Bible, means our brotherly and spiritual love for one another harmonizing with God's great love for us.

It is this spirit of charity we should cultivate in place of vindictive thoughts. And we can be helped to do so, when we read:

> And now abideth faith, hope, charity, these three; but the greatest of these is charity.
>
> I CORINTHIANS 13:13

> And though I bestow all my goods to feed the poor, and though I give my body to be burned, and have not charity, it profiteth me nothing.
> Charity suffereth long, and is kind; charity envieth not; charity vaunteth not itself, is not puffed up,
> Doth not behave itself unseemly, seeketh not her own, is not easily provoked, thinketh no evil;
> Rejoiceth not in iniquity, but rejoiceth in the truth.
>
> I CORINTHIANS 13:3–6

A heart filled with anger is a heart without joy, and this joyless heart leads us to believe that we have the right to judge others, and the right to avenge ourselves on those who have wronged us; but the Bible tells us that these are the prerogatives of the Lord:

> But let him that glorieth glory in this, that he understandeth and knoweth me, that I am the Lord which exercise loving-kindness, judgment, and righteousness, in the earth: for in these things I delight, saith the Lord.
>
> JEREMIAH 9:24

Thou shalt not avenge, nor bear any grudge against the children of thy people, but thou shalt love thy neighbor as thyself: I am the Lord.

LEVITICUS 19:18

Bless them which persecute you: bless, and curse not.

ROMANS 12:14

Do you harbor thoughts of revenge in your heart? You may be able to fool all those around you into believing that you are a loving person, but you cannot fool our Creator:

Every way of a man is right in his own eyes: but the Lord pondereth the hearts.

PROVERBS 21:2

The next time you long for revenge, but yet feel torn, because you know that this is not Jesus' way, remember His words at Calvary:

Then said Jesus, Father, forgive them; for they know not what they do. And they parted his raiment, and cast lots.

LUKE 23:34

Sickness, Suffering and Pain

Do you know anyone at all who has gone through life without knowing some sickness? If he hasn't suffered illness personally, someone in his family, or a beloved friend, may have been afflicted by a debilitating disease. And for most of us, seeing those we love in pain is worse than suffering the pain ourselves.

Who can we turn to when we suffer from sickness and pain? Doctors offer hope, medicines alleviate some of the agonies. But for true, spiritual comfort, for inner fortitude, we must turn to God's Word.

Physicians may be able to lessen bodily pain, but it is our Lord and His Son who help us when physical illness makes us soul weary and sick at heart. As the poet Alexander Pope said,

> All are but parts of one stupendous whole,
> Whose body Nature is, and God the soul.

> The spirit of a man will sustain his infirmity; but a wounded spirit who can bear?
> PROVERBS 18:14

Perhaps when you are among family and friends, you try to make them feel better by pretending that you are not suffering as much as you really are. But this bravery cannot continue, and often when you are alone, you give in to your tears of pain.

Don't be ashamed of expressing these feelings. Doctors

today advise their patients to be honest about the emotions they experience during illness; they say this has a therapeutic effect. The Bible said that a long time ago:

> Be afflicted, and mourn, and weep: let your laughter be turned to mourning, and your joy to heaviness.
> Humble yourselves in the sight of the Lord, and he shall lift you up.
>
> JAMES 4:9–10

God wants you to be honest with Him. He wants you to come to Him when you are ill, or faint, or weary. The prophet Isaiah relates the story of King Hezekiah:

> In those days was Hezekiah sick unto death. And Isaiah the prophet the son of Amoz came unto him, and said unto him, Thus saith the Lord, Set thine house in order: for thou shalt die, and not live.
> Then Hezekiah turned his face toward the wall, and prayed unto the Lord,
> And said, Remember now, O Lord, I beseech thee, how I have walked before thee in truth and with a perfect heart, and have done that which is good in thy sight. And Hezekiah wept sore.
> Then came the word of the Lord to Isaiah, saying,
> Go, and say to Hezekiah, Thus saith the Lord, the God of David thy father, I have heard thy prayer, I have seen thy tears: behold, I will add unto thy days fifteen years.
>
> ISAIAH 38:1–5

Psychologically, it is a good idea to reveal your suffering. Relief can come even as the words burst out of you, "I'm in pain—I need help."

The Bible teaches us that men have turned to God for solace and that He has held them in His hands, even as He listens and strengthens them:

> O Lord, rebuke me not in thine anger, neither chasten me in thy hot displeasure.
>
> Have mercy upon me, O Lord; for I am weak: O Lord, heal me; for my bones are vexed.
>
> My soul is also sore vexed: but thou, O Lord, how long?
>
> Return, O Lord, deliver my soul: oh save me for thy mercies' sake.
>
> PSALMS 6:1–4

You have prayed for help, you have asked the One on High to hear you. You now feel easier in your heart because you have shared your problems.

You would, of course, thank a doctor who prescribed for you, or a psychiatrist who heard you. Do not forget to thank the Great Listener and Healer:

> The living, the living, he shall praise thee, as I do this day: the father to the children shall make known thy truth.
>
> The Lord was ready to save me: therefore we will sing my songs to the stringed instruments all the days of our life in the house of the Lord.
>
> ISAIAH 38:19–20

> Depart from me, all ye workers of iniquity; for the Lord hath hea d the voice of my weeping.
>
> The Lord hath heard my supplication; the Lord will receive my prayer.
>
> Let all mine enemies be ashamed and sore vexed: let them return and be ashamed suddenly.
>
> PSALMS 6:8–10

If you've ever been ill, you know the great weariness of the soul that overtakes you. You have taken your medicine, you are doing what doctors tell you to do, yet recovery seems to be so slow.

Remember, that while you may tire, God does not. He

watches over you. Continue the treatment, take your medicines without fail, and add to it the healing prescription of faith:

> Hast thou not known? Hast thou not heard, that the everlasting God, the Lord, the Creator of the ends of the earth, fainteth not, neither is weary? There is no searching of his understanding.
>
> He giveth power to the faint; and to them that have no might he increaseth strength.
>
> Even the youths shall faint and be weary, and the young men shall utterly fall:
>
> But they that wait upon the Lord shall renew their strength; they shall mount up with wings as eagles; they shall run, and not be weary; and they shall walk, and not faint.
>
> ISAIAH 40:28–31

Through the centuries, many physicians have named the Son of God the Great Physician, and the Bible gives ample proof of our Saviour's power of healing. The Gospel tells us that:

> And in that same hour he cured many of their infirmities and plagues, and of evil spirits; and unto many that were blind he gave sight.
>
> Then Jesus answering said unto them, Go your way, and tell John what things ye have seen and heard; how that the blind see, the lame walk, the lepers are cleansed, the deaf hear, the dead are raised, to the poor the gospel is preached.
>
> LUKE 7:21–22

Our Lord Jesus has compassion on everyone. He is beside you now, wanting to comfort you in your suffering. Let Him treat your soul. Remember how Jesus quieted the wild waves of the sea? He can also quiet you:

And when he was entered into a ship, his disciples followed him.

And, behold, there arose a great tempest in the sea, insomuch that the ship was covered with the waves: but he was asleep.

And his disciples came to him, and awoke him, saying, Lord save us: we perish.

And he saith unto them, Why are ye fearful, O ye of little faith? Then he arose and rebuked the winds and the sea; and there was a great calm.

MATTHEW 8:23–26

Doctors know that a calm spirit, a clear mind are important in making someone well. There is a tremendous interaction between our minds and our bodies. As we relax, have faith, gain spiritual strength from our beliefs, our bodies will also regain their strength. A fretful spirit can retard recovery:

A merry heart doeth good like a medicine: but a broken spirit drieth the bones.

PROVERBS 17:22

Perhaps you're thinking that you are too sick just now to have a *merry* heart. Your heart is too burdened, you are too full of pain. In that case, share your burden—it will seem lighter. Do you tell your family just how you feel? Your doctor? Your friends? Come to God with your pain; do not wait to speak out:

And now, Lord, what wait I for? My hope is in thee.

Deliver me from all my transgressions: make me not the reproach of the foolish.

I was dumb, I opened not my mouth; because thou didst it.

Remove thy stroke away from me: I am consumed by the blow of thine hand.

PSALMS 39:7–10

The Bible tells us to come openly to the Lord. He knows us, He cares for us, He will help us:

> Come, and let us return unto the Lord: for he hath torn, and he will heal us; he hath smitten, and he will bind us up.
>
> HOSEA 6:1

> O Lord my God, I cried unto thee, and thou hast healed me.
>
> O Lord, thou hast brought up my soul from the grave: thou hast kept me alive, that I should not go down to the pit.
>
> Sing unto the Lord, O ye saints of his, and give thanks at the remembrance of his holiness.
>
> For his anger endureth but a moment; in his favor is life: weeping may endure for a night, but joy cometh in the morning.
>
> PSALMS 30:2–5

> Heal me, O Lord, and I shall be healed; save me, and I shall be saved: for thou art my praise.
>
> JEREMIAH 17:14

Never forget that in your trouble and trial you are never alone. Lean on our Lord Jesus, let Him lay His Hands on you and help your soul regain its strength:

> Now when the sun was setting, all they that had any sick with divers diseases brought them unto him; and he laid his hands on every one of them, and healed them.
>
> And devils also came out of many, crying out, and saying, Thou art Christ the Son of God. And he rebuking them suffered them not to speak: for they knew that he was Christ.
>
> LUKE 4:40–41

Sin and Guilt

You've done something wrong, something really bad. At first, you may try to discount your actions with, "Oh, well, it wasn't that bad," or, "Everyone does the same thing, so why should I worry?"

But, because in the past you have felt happy and warm basking in the love of Christ, you do feel bad. Perhaps you have broken a law of man, and committed a crime, or maybe you have transgressed one of God's laws, and committed a sin.

Your sin suddenly looms large before you; it is like a wall separating you from God. You may be surrounded by people, but with that wall around you, you feel lonely and lost. You want to come to Jesus again, you want to enjoy that spiritual communion you once knew, but you fear that this will never be possible for you again.

You are suffering from guilt, a guilt so large that it prevents you from enjoying even simple, everyday pleasures. If you let this guilt take hold of your life, it can actually make you physically ill.

Before you are drawn deeper into this morass of guilt, remember that Jesus Christ died for us so that we may be cleansed of sin. If we admit that we've done wrong, and are truly repentant, Jesus will welcome us, and lead us back to our Father.

But before that can happen, we must openly admit our wrongdoing, and humbly ask to be forgiven. If in your unhappiness and confusion you can't find the right words, turn to the Book of Psalms, and repeat the prayer of a penitent King David:

> Have mercy upon me, O God, according to thy loving-kindness: according unto the multitude of thy tender mercies blot out my transgressions.
>
> Wash me thoroughly from mine iniquity, and cleanse me from my sin.
>
> For I acknowledge my transgressions; and my sin is ever before me.
>
> Against thee, thee only, have I sinned, and done this evil in thy sight: that thou mightest be justified when thou speakest, and be clear when thou judgest.
>
> PSALMS 51:1-4

Is it true? Can you dare to believe that Lord Jesus Christ will actually save you, no matter what you have done? God's Holy Word assures and reassures us of this very fact:

> For the Son of man is come to save that which was lost.
>
> MATTHEW 18:11

You may know such shame, such guilt, that you hesitate to go to gentle Jesus. But He will give you the strength so that you can come to Him, because only through His intercession can you also return to our Father:

> For there is one God, and one mediator between God and men, the man Christ Jesus.
>
> I TIMOTHY 2:5

If you wonder that God can allow a sinner such as yourself to return to His side, be comforted by yet another proof of God's great love for you:

> But God commendeth his love toward us, in that, while we were yet sinners, Christ died for us.
>
> ROMANS 5:8

And because of His great sacrifice, we can be freed from our sin if we come to Him. We do not have to carry the burden of our sin forever:

> For sin shall not have dominion over you: for ye are not under the law, but under grace.
>
> ROMANS 6:14

Let your faith return to you; your belief in Christ's sacrifice can overcome your feelings of guilt. Even before the birth of Christ, Isaiah prophesied that we would be washed clean in the Blood of the Lamb:

> Come now, and let us reason together, saith the Lord: though your sins be as scarlet, they shall be as white as snow; though they be red like crimson, they shall be as wool.
>
> ISAIAH 1:18

And the wonderful truth of that prophecy finally came to pass, as the Scriptures make it clear to us:

> For when we were yet without strength, in due time Christ died for the ungodly.
> For scarcely for a righteous man will one die: yet peradventure for a good man some would even dare to die.
> But God commendeth his love toward us, in that, while we were yet sinners, Christ died for us.
> Much more then, being now justified by his blood, we shall be saved from wrath through him.
> For if, when we were enemies, we were reconciled to God by the death of his Son, much more, being reconciled, we shall be saved by his life.
> And not only so, but we also joy in God through our

Lord Jesus Christ, by whom we have now received the atonement.

ROMANS 5:6–11

You have repented, and been forgiven, and slowly you begin to experience a wonderful sense of tranquility. Through Christ, you have come close to God once again, and your soul is at peace.

What a wonderful, loving gift you have received! What can you do to express your gratitude? God's Word presents many reminders of the great blessing that has been given to us, and as we read these passages, we hope that they will help us to be less sinful in the future:

Surely he hath borne our griefs, and carried our sorrows: yet we did esteem him stricken, smitten of God, and afflicted.

But he was wounded for our transgressions, he was bruised for our iniquities: the chastisement of our peace was upon him; and with his stripes we are healed.

All we like sheep have gone astray; we have turned every one to his own way; and the Lord hath laid on him the iniquity of us all.

ISAIAH 53:4–6

Jesus sorrows each time we sin anew, and knowing this, we ask His help in guiding our feet on righteous paths:

Lord, I cry unto thee: make haste unto me; give ear unto my voice, when I cry unto thee.

Let my prayer be set forth before thee as incense; and the lifting up of my hands as the evening sacrifice.

Set a watch, O Lord, before my mouth; keep the door of my lips.

Incline not my heart to any evil thing, to practice wicked works with men that work iniquity: and let me not eat of their dainties.

PSALMS 141:1–4

No man is perfect. The Bible confirms this:

> Who can say, I have made my heart clean, I am pure
> from my sin?
>
> PROVERBS 20:9

We can't be perfect, but we can try to be better; this is
what He asks from us. And even as we try, we do falter,
but He sees our efforts, and His pity and forgiveness are
infinite:

> My little children, these things write I unto you, that
> ye sin not. And if any man sin, we have an advocate with
> the Father, Jesus Christ the righteous:
> And he is the propitiation for our sins: and not for
> ours only, but also for the sins of the whole world.
>
> I JOHN 2:1–2

Some people feel so burdened with sin and guilt that
they think of God as they might think of an accountant:
tallying up their virtues and their weaknesses, and keeping a strict account.

But those who walk with Jesus, recognizing Him as the
Redeemer, know that they will not be so judged, because
through our Saviour even a page heavily covered with a
list of sins can be completely erased:

> I, even I, am he that blotteth out thy transgressions
> for mine own sake, and will not remember thy sins.
>
> ISAIAH 43:25

> And they shall teach no more every man his neighbor,
> and every man his brother, saying, Know the Lord: for
> they shall all know me, from the least of them unto the
> greatest of them, saith the Lord: for I will forgive their
> iniquity, and I will remember their sin no more.
>
> JEREMIAH 31:34

God's Holy Word offers much comfort when we read and understand how very much He wants to forgive us and have us enjoy life eternal with His Son:

> But if the wicked will turn from all his sins that he hath committed, and keep all my statutes, and do that which is lawful and right, he shall surely live, he shall not die.
>
> All his transgressions that he hath committed, they shall not be mentioned unto him: in his righteousness that he hath done he shall live.
>
> Have I any pleasure at all that the wicked should die? saith the Lord God: and not that he should return from his ways, and live?
>
> EZEKIAL 18:21–23

> Therefore I will judge you, O house of Israel, every one according to his ways, saith the Lord God. Repent, and turn yourselves from all your transgressions; so iniquity shall not be your ruin.
>
> Cast away from you all your transgressions, whereby ye have transgressed; and make you a new heart and a new spirit: for why will ye die, O house of Israel?
>
> For I have no pleasure in the death of him that dieth, saith the Lord God: wherefore turn yourselves, and live ye.
>
> EZEKIAL 18:30–32

> He that followeth after righteousness and mercy findeth life, righteousness, and honor.
>
> PROVERBS 21:21

Being forgiven when we sin, and having guilt removed from us, does not mean that we are dealing with a permissive God. We must recognize His absolute authority and accept His anger when we transgress against Him, understanding that He has the power to both chastise and heal:

> Behold, happy is the man whom God correcteth:
> therefore despise not thou the chastening of the Al-
> mighty:
> For he maketh sore, and bindeth up: he woundeth,
> and his hands make whole.
>
> JOB 5:17–18

Falling into sin can be likened to falling ill; sinning is a moral and a spiritual illness, and we can be helped toward health by our Saviour:

> And, behold, there was a woman which had a spirit of
> infirmity eighteen years, and was bowed together, and
> could in no wise lift up herself.
> And when Jesus saw her, he called her to him, and
> said unto her, Woman, thou art loosed from thine in-
> firmity.
> And he laid his hands on her: and immediately she
> was made straight, and glorified God.
>
> LUKE 13:11–13

In the same way, Jesus comes to you, lays His Hand upon you, and cures you of your spiritual illness.

The Holy Scriptures comfort us with His understanding. He knows that, hard as we try to avoid it, there are many ways we can be led into sin:

> For we wrestle not against flesh and blood, but against
> principalities, against powers, against the rulers of dark-
> ness of this world, against spiritual wickedness in high
> places.
> Wherefore take unto you the whole armor of God,
> that ye may be able to withstand in the evil day, and
> having done all, to stand.
>
> EPHESIANS 6:12–13

Should you sin again, do not let dire feelings of guilt overwhelm you. Do not fall into a pit of anxiety and depression. Instead of letting the emotions rule you, lean on your positive faith in the power of our Saviour to redeem you.

Never forget that He died so that we may be saved. Remember that His Hand is always stretched out to you with compassion and with forgiveness. Let His strong Hand grip your weak one, and He will raise you up. He has done this for you so many times before, and He will do it again:

> The next day John seeth Jesus coming unto him, and saith, Behold the Lamb of God, which taketh away the sin of the world!
>
> JOHN 1:29

Sorrow and Anguish

You wake up in the morning, and you get dressed. You have breakfast, and you go about your day's work. The hours pass, but though the sun may be shining outside of your window, your soul does not feel involved in the brightness without, because your mood is a solemn gray.

You are gripped by such sorrow that every sound, every voice, seems muffled and far away. If music was once a comfort, it seems to have lost its harmonious effect; if looking out at God's landscape was once a great pleasure, you have lost the ability to see the beauty around you.

There is no one who has not been through such periods of sorrow, such days of anguish. They may be rooted in a variety of experiences: the loss of a loved one through death, the coldness of an old friend, the loss of a job, the feeling that life is passing us by, the inability to have a child, the sensation that meaning has gone out of life, extreme weariness from overwork coupled with the belief that your efforts are unappreciated.

The next time you go through a period of such wrechedness that your spirit is crushed, turn to God's Holy Word where you will find much to strengthen you:

> Hear my cry, O God; attend unto my prayer.
> From the end of the earth will I cry unto thee, when my heart is overwhelmed; lead me to the rock that is higher than I.
> For thou hast been a shelter for me, and a strong tower from the enemy.

I will abide in thy tabernacle for ever: I will trust in the covert of thy wings. Selah.

PSALMS 61:1-4

When your spirit is weakest, when you feel sure that you can't make it through the day, remember the promise made to all those who sorrow:

The righteous cry, and the Lord heareth, and delivereth them out of all their troubles.

The Lord is nigh unto them that are of a broken heart; and saveth such as be of a contrite spirit.

PSALMS 34:17-18

Perhaps, even at this moment, you are thinking that no one understands you, because no one has suffered as you are suffering now. But this is not so; others have experienced terrible times of anguish. The Bible tells us of the suffering of Job which was so great that his friends had no words with which they could comfort him:

So they sat down with him upon the ground seven days and seven nights, and none spake a word unto him: for they saw that his grief was very great.

JOB 2:13

And when Job found words, he spoke about the heaviness, the weight of his misery:

But Job answered and said,

Oh that my grief were thoroughly weighed, and my calamity laid in the balances together!

For now it would be heavier than the sand of the sea: therefore my words are swallowed up.

JOB 6:1-3

In time, according to God's Plan, Job was comforted and even rewarded, and if you are faithful to Him, He will heed your cry when He decides it is time to do so:

And therefore will the Lord wait, that he may be gracious unto you, and therefore will he be exalted, that he may have mercy upon you: for the Lord is a God of Judgment: blessed are all they that wait for him.

For the people shall dwell in Zion at Jerusalem: thou shalt weep no more: he will be very gracious unto thee at the voice of thy cry; when he shall hear it, he will answer thee.

ISAIAH 30:18–19

Of course, it is hard to wait for God's graciousness. You are impatient and filled with pain. The Bible will help you to understand that others have felt as you feel now. You are not alone:

Is it nothing to you, all ye that pass by? Behold, and see if there be any sorrow like unto my sorrow, which is done unto me, wherewith the Lord hath afflicted me in the day of his fierce anger.

LAMENTATIONS 1:12

Ask yourself what you have done to incur God's holy anger, always remembering that He does not act toward you with vindictiveness, because as His Book tells us:

For he doth not afflict willingly nor grieve the children of men.

LAMENTATIONS 3:33

Turn to God, admit your faults, and express your hope and faith in Him:

Why art thou cast down, O my soul? And why art thou disquieted in me? Hope thou in God: for I shall yet praise him for the help of his countenance.

PSALMS 42:5

It does take a great deal of faith to continue to hope when you are suffering anguish, but God's Book offers many wonderful examples of those who never lost their faith, no matter how sorely they were tried and tested. Let their faith bolster your own:

> Take, my brethren, the prophets, who have spoken in the name of the Lord, for an example of suffering affliction, and of patience.
>
> Behold, we count them happy which endure. Ye have heard of the patience of Job, and have seen the end of the Lord; that the Lord is very pitiful, and of tender mercy.
>
> JAMES 5:10–11

The Bible advises us to turn toward the Lord with our prayers at all times:

> Is any among you afflicted? Let him pray. Is any merry? Let him sing psalms.
>
> Is any sick among you? Let him call for the elders of the church; and let them pray over him, anointing him with oil in the name of the Lord.
>
> JAMES 5:13–14

Can you doubt that you will be heard? We are promised again and again that our prayers will be answered, sorrow removed from us, and that we will be happy once again when we pray to Him and ask for help in His blessed Son's name:

> Hitherto have ye asked nothing in my name: ask, and ye shall receive, that your joy may be full.
>
> JOHN 16:24

Our Saviour, who suffered such anguish for our sakes, does not want your sorrow to be endless. He knows that, even though you are experiencing pain at this time, you will experience happiness once again—the happiness that comes to all who believe in Him:

Verily, verily, I say unto you, That ye shall weep and lament, but the world shall rejoice: and ye shall be sorrowful, but your sorrow shall be turned into joy.

A woman when she is in travail hath sorrow, because her hour is come: but as soon as she is delivered of the child, she remembereth no more the anguish, for joy that a man is born into the world.

And ye now therefore have sorrow: but I will see you again, and your heart shall rejoice, and your joy no man taketh from you.

JOHN 16:20–22

Are you one of those people who are most faithful when everything is going right for you? Perhaps your present tribulations are a testing of your faith. Try to compose your spirit and believe in His compassion. Turn toward God, humbly asking His help:

Yea, for thy sake are we killed all the day long; we are counted as sheep for the slaughter.

Awake, why sleepest thou, O Lord? Arise, cast us not off for ever.

Wherefore hidest thou thy face, and forgettest our affliction and our oppression?

For our soul is bowed down to the dust: our belly cleaveth unto the earth.

Arise for our help, and redeem us for thy mercies' sake.

PSALMS 44:22–26

It is not up to us to question His ways; we must respect God's Plan even though it is not always given to us to understand it.

If you're having a really bad time, remember that you are one with Jesus Christ, and in some measure you are sharing His suffering:

Beloved, think it not strange concerning the fiery trial which is to try you, as though some strange thing happened unto you:

But rejoice, inasmuch as ye are partakers of Christ's sufferings; that, when his glory shall be revealed, ye may be glad also with exceeding joy.

I PETER 4:12–13

You will be able to bear all sorrows more easily if you accept God in all His omnipotence. It may seem that you are wandering in circles, or in a strange maze, but believe that He sees you from on high, and is directing your steps.

He is aware of everything that happens on His earth, even to the last, smallest blade of grass:

> The voice of him that crieth in the wilderness, Prepare ye the way of the Lord, make straight in the desert a highway for our God.
>
> Every valley shall be exalted, and every mountain and hill shall be made low: and the crooked shall be made straight, and the rough places plain:
>
> And the glory of the Lord shall be revealed, and all flesh shall see it together: for the mouth of the Lord hath spoken it.
>
> The voice said, Cry. And he said, What shall I cry? All flesh is grass, and all the goodliness thereof is as the flower of the field:
>
> The grass withereth, the flower fadeth: because the spirit of the Lord bloweth upon it: surely the people is grass.
>
> The grass withereth, the flower fadeth: but the word of our God shall stand for ever.

ISAIAH 40:3–8

The days seem less gray; you understand that your sorrow will come to an end as you read these words proving that God has never turned from you. Men may ignore you, they may not want to know you when you are troubled, but this is never true of our Creator:

> Are not two sparrows sold for a farthing? And one of them shall not fall on the ground without your Father.

But the very hairs of your head are all numbered.
Fear ye not therefore, ye are of more value than many sparrows.

MATTHEW 10:29–31

The Bible tells us that at times we must know misery so that we can better understand His anguish and come closer to our Saviour through our sorrow:

Behold, I have refined thee, but not with silver; I have chosen thee in the furnace of affliction.

ISAIAH 48:10

Therefore I take pleasure in infirmities, in reproaches, in necessities, in persecutions, in distresses for Christ's sake: for when I am weak, then am I strong.

II CORINTHIANS 12:10

Haven't you found that the people who are most sympathetic, most understanding, are those who have suffered and known distress? Experiencing sorrow can make us more compassionate toward others. We are most likely to hold out a hand to those in pain, when we, too, have known pain. This may be a reason for the anguish you are going through right now.

However, never doubt that your pain will come to an end. Raise your voice in prayer to our Lord. Say these words out loud:

Forsake me not, O Lord: O my God, be not far from me.
Make haste to help me, O Lord my salvation.

PSALMS 38:21–22

The Scriptures tell us again and again that He hears us and will make us happy and spiritually whole once again:

He healeth the broken in heart, and bindeth up their wounds.

PSALMS 147:3

Sorrow will depart from your heart and anguish from your soul when you read in God's Holy Word that Jesus loves you, and wants you to spend eternity with Him:

> Father, I will that they also, whom thou hast given me, be with me where I am; that they may behold my glory, which thou hast given me: for thou lovedst me before the foundation of the world.
>
> O righteous Father, the world hath not known thee: but I have known thee, and these have known that thou hast sent me.
>
> And I have declared unto them thy name, and will declare it: that the love wherewith thou hast loved me may be in them, and I in them.

JOHN 17:24–26

Stress and Tension

The times we live in have more than their quota of stress and tension-producing situations. Each day, our nerves and our bodies and our minds are assaulted by many strains.

Police sirens and ambulance bells seem louder than ever. Cities have become more packed, and the spillover of extra people is now making suburbs and rural areas more crowded.

There is the pressure of world events, which affects all of us. We worry about war, about jobs, about even having enough money to make ends meet, about ever-rising prices, and about the wisdom of our investments.

With all the ecological problems that surround us, we know that there are many factors outside of our control that threaten our health and the health of those we love.

Frequently, we are apprehensive about the very food we eat, worrying about additives. Yet other times we worry about the people who don't have enough food to meet their needs.

We are surrounded by people who are as subject to tensions and stresses as we are, and frequently they over-react and treat us with anger and rudeness, evoking our angry spirit in turn.

Very often, we feel as though we were walking a high tightrope; we are fearful of falling into the abyss of nervous illness; and physical symptoms, too, can be the result of too much stress. Hypertension and high blood pressure are common ailments today; there's the fear of tension-created heart problems; and we know of many people who won't start the day without doctor-prescribed tranquilizing pills.

Some days, when we take off a little time to think about our lives, we know that this is surely not the way God intended us to live. But most of the time, we are just too busy trying to get through each day to try to figure out how we can make the next twenty-four hours better. As the poet William Wordsworth wrote:

> The world is too much with us; late and soon,
> Getting and spending, we lay waste our powers:
> Little we see in Nature that is ours.

But the time comes, finally, when we realize that if we don't separate ourselves somewhat from the physical world, don't give more attention to our spiritual needs, we will reach a state of such intense emotional strain that we will have to take to our beds, completely unable to cope.

We understand the need to relax, we recognize the importance of finding more time to develop healthier, spiritual selves, but we have lived with stress situations for so long that we don't know how to work our way out of them.

This is the time to turn to God's Word. Here, in the Bible written thousands of years ago, you will find the answers to today's problems. The Scriptures tell us that though we see trouble on all sides, we have not been abandoned:

> We are troubled on every side, yet not distressed; we
> are perplexed, but not in despair;
> Persecuted, but not forsaken; cast down, but not de-
> stroyed.
>
> II CORINTHIANS 4:8–9

Stress and tension usually result in apprehension. Sometimes we can't even give a name to our terrors, and it is these nameless fears that are the worst.

If you frequently experience a sense of anxiety that leaves you with a pounding pulse and a dry mouth, turn to the prophet Isaiah. These words will help restore your spirit:

> And it shall come to pass in the day that the Lord shall give thee rest from thy sorrow, and from thy fear, and from the hard bondage wherein thou wast made to serve.
>
> ISAIAH 14:3

Doctors often advise their patients who are suffering from the effects of extreme tension to try to step away from themselves. It isn't easy to do, but they suggest that these patients avoid pessimistic thoughts and do their best to cultivate a sense of humor about themselves and their problems. This conforms with what we're told in God's Word:

> A merry heart maketh a cheerful countenance: but by sorrow of the heart the spirit is broken.
>
> PROVERBS 15:13

However, there are some days when those words just don't reach you. You can't smile—you can't even pretend to smile—when what you really want to do is run away and hide. When you feel that way, run away to the refuge offered you by our Lord:

> He that dwelleth in the secret place of the most High shall abide under the shadow of the Almighty.
> I will say of the Lord, He is my refuge and my fortress: my God; in him will I trust.
> Surely he shall deliver thee from the snare of the fowler, and from the noisome pestilence.

He shall cover thee with his feathers, and under his wings shalt thou trust: his truth shall be thy shield and buckler.

Thou shalt not be afraid for the terror by night; nor for the arrow that flieth by day;

Nor for the pestilence that walketh in darkness; nor for the destruction that wasteth at noonday.

A thousand shall fall at thy side, and ten thousand at thy right hand; but it shall not come nigh thee.

Only with thine eyes shalt thou behold and see the reward of the wicked.

Because thou hast made the Lord, which is my refuge, even the most High, thy habitation;

There shall no evil befall thee, neither shall any plague come nigh thy dwelling.

For he shall give his angels charge over thee, to keep thee in all thy ways.

They shall bear thee up in their hands, lest thou dash thy foot against a stone.

PSALMS 91:1—12

Reading that Psalm over and over again gives you a chance to breathe deeply. You begin to think, and you take time to assess your life. Is there something you can do to eliminate tension-producing situations? Perhaps you have been giving too much emphasis to things of material value and not enough to your soul. If this is so, remember the words of our Saviour:

For what is a man profited, if he shall gain the whole world, and lose his own soul? Or what shall a man give in exchange for his soul?

MATTHEW 16:26

Have you put too much emphasis on possessions, and not enough on riches of the spirit? God's Word tells us that it is frequently better to have less—less money, less furniture, less clothes, less cars; sometimes an abundance of things creates a screen between us and the truly important possessions of spiritual value:

> Better is a handful with quietness, than both the hands full with travail and vexation of spirit.
>
> ECCLESIASTES 4:6

> As sorrowful, yet always rejoicing; as poor, yet making many rich; as having nothing, and yet possessing all things.
>
> II CORINTHIANS 6:10

Let us say that you are determined to lessen the tension in your life. You intend to change those things that can be changed for the better, and to accept those things which cannot be changed. But it is hard to accept certain things. You see the need for improvement, yet you can do nothing. You become more and more frustrated, and as your frustrations increase, so do all the terrible symptoms of your tension-filled life.

Sit back, relax, understand that the ability to change things is not always in your hands. Instead of trying to do everything yourself, turn to the Lord, and seek His help. God wants you to do the work of this world with peace in your heart. He does not want your days to be so filled with stress that you cannot enjoy His gifts here on His earth:

> I have seen the travail, which God hath given to the sons of men to be exercised in it.
>
> He hath made every thing beautiful in his time: also he hath set the world in their heart, so that no man can find out the work that God maketh from the beginning to the end.
>
> I know that there is no good in them, but for a man to rejoice, and to do good in his life.
>
> And also that every man should eat and drink, and enjoy the good of all his labor, it is the gift of God.
>
> ECCLESIASTES 3:10–13

In recent years, many religious and quasi-psychological cults have sprung up. All of them aver that they can cure the modern ills of tension. Some recommend turning to Eastern religions and learning to meditate; others proffer aggressive behavior; still others insist that the only way to find inner peace is to return to infancy and scream away our troubles.

But God's help is waiting for you in God's Book. Pray to Him, meditate about Him, start every morning with this prayer, and your days may suddenly be filled with a new and wonderful measure of peace:

> Give ear to my words, O Lord; consider me meditation.
> Hearken unto the voice of my cry, my King, and my God: for unto thee will I pray.
> My voice shalt thou hear in the morning, O Lord; in the morning will I direct my prayer unto thee, and will look up.
>
> PSALMS 5:1-3

Don't be fooled by cults and fads. They may say that they can relieve your state of emotional strain with some brand-new idea, but all good ideas stem from God's Holy Word. And if your confidence is for the very new, remember that we are born anew with our belief in Jesus Christ:

> Therefore, if any man be in Christ, he is a new creature: old things are passed away; behold, all things are become new.
>
> II CORINTHIANS 5:17

There are some mornings when you just can't seem to get out of bed. Tension has so fatigued you that you don't want to face another day. But place your faith in Jesus. Ask Him to accompany you as you go through the day, and you will know that He will walk beside you. He will give you courage and renew that inner man within you:

> We having the same spirit of faith, according as it is written, I believed, and therefore have I spoken; we also believe, and therefore speak;
> Knowing that he which raised up the Lord Jesus shall raise up us also by Jesus, and shall present us with you.
> For all things are for your sakes, that the abundant grace might through the thanksgiving of many redound to the glory of God.
> For which cause we faint not; but though our outward man perish, yet the inward man is renewed day by day.
>
> II CORINTHIANS 4:13–16

God's Word warns us that we must not let the cares of the day so obsess us that we forget the spiritual light of Jesus which has been given to us. One way to lessen stress-caused problems is to give more concentration to our Saviour's words:

> Take heed therefore that the light which is in thee be not darkness.
> If thy whole body therefore be full of light, having no part dark, the whole shall be full of light, as when the bright shining of a candle doth give thee light.
>
> LUKE 11:35–36

After a day's work do you suffer from a tension headache, or a tension backache, or perhaps a tension heartache—meaning a diminishing of your usually peaceful spirit?

If these are familiar complaints, and you've consulted a physician who has used the words "tension-induced symptoms," and who has suggested that you try to relax, pay attention to him.

One way to relax is to sit down in a quiet room in your

own home. Find a comfortable chair, put your feet up, turn on a good reading light, and then turn to the light of the Bible. God's Word will help reduce the day's tension, and go far toward alleviating stress:

> Finally, brethren, farewell. Be perfect, be of good comfort, be of one mind, live in peace; and the God of love and peace shall be with you.
> Greet one another with a holy kiss.
> All the saints salute you.
> The grace of the Lord Jesus Christ, and the love of God, and the communion of the Holy Ghost, be with you all. Amen.
>
> II CORINTHIANS 13:11–14

Temptation

Temptations surround us on all sides. They come in all sizes and shapes; some of them are just a little tempting, others are so seductive and alluring that they lead us far from the paths we know we should walk. As the seventeenth-century author, Matthew Henry, wrote:

> Many a dangerous temptation comes to us in fine gay colors that are but skin-deep.

All of us have our own list of temptations, and very often we try to keep this list secret. Our temptations may range from something as slight as the desire to eat too much chocolate cake, to more serious enticements, such as gambling, or the carnal urge to possess a woman or a man who is not our spouse.

Some people are tempted by money, or the desire for revenge; others are tempted by power or a need to succeed that is so powerful it overrules all sense of fair play and decency.

Temptations can't be avoided: you can't pretend that the bakery won't sell you a pecan pie; you can't shut your eyes to the beauty of another man's wife or to the handsomeness of another woman's husband. Gambling tables exist, and card games do take place.

But while you can't ignore the existence of temptations, you can fight them with spiritual strength. The Holy Scriptures offer help to all those who truly want to say "No!" to evil enticements.

Perhaps you think that our Saviour cannot help you, but remember that He, too, was tempted:

> Then was Jesus led up of the spirit into the wilderness to be tempted of the devil.
>
> And when he had fasted forty days and forty nights, he was afterward ahungered.
>
> And when the tempter came to him, he said, If thou be the Son of God, command that these stones be made bread.
>
> But he answered and said, It is written, Man shall not live by bread alone, but by every word that proceedeth out of the mouth of God.
>
> Then the devil taketh him up into the holy city, and setteth him on a pinnacle of the temple,
>
> And saith unto him, If thou be the Son of God, cast thyself down: for it is written, He shall give his angels charge concerning thee: and in their hands they shall bear thee up, lest at any time thou dash thy foot against a stone.
>
> Jesus said unto him, It is written again, Thou shalt not tempt the Lord thy God.
>
> Again, the devil taketh him up into an exceeding high mountain, and showeth him all the kingdoms of the world, and the glory of them;
>
> And saith unto him, All these things will I give thee, if thou wilt fall down and worship me.
>
> Then saith Jesus unto him, Get thee hence, Satan: for it is written, Thou shalt worship the Lord thy God, and him only shalt thou serve.
>
> Then the devil leaveth him, and, behold, angels came and ministered unto him.

MATTHEW 4:1–11

Understand that our Lord Jesus is aware of everything. He knows of the beauties and wonders of Heaven, and He also knows what you face here on earth:

> For in that he himself hath suffered being tempted, he is able to succor them that are tempted.

HEBREWS 2:18

When you face allurements that you cannot ignore, consult the Holy Scriptures and pray for the guidance necessary to keep your feet from slipping:

> Truly God is good to Israel, even to such as are of a clean heart.
> But as for me, my feet were almost gone; my steps had well-nigh slipped.
> For I was envious at the foolish, when I saw the prosperity of the wicked.
>
> PSALMS 73:1–3

The Bible instructs us not to envy the sinners who have succumbed to temptation; their lives can end only in unhappiness:

> Hear thou, my son, and be wise, and guide thine heart in the way.
> Be not among winebibbers; among riotous eaters of the flesh:
> For the drunkard and the glutton shall come to poverty: and the drowsiness shall clothe a man with rags.
>
> PROVERBS 23:19–21

Often we are tempted, and very often we give in to temptation. We then feel shame before our Lord and His Son. Turn to God, and let the Psalms help you to express your feelings of regret for what you have done:

> So foolish was I, and ignorant: I was as a beast before thee.
> Nevertheless I am continually with thee: thou hast holden me by my right hand.
> Thou shalt guide me with thy counsel, and afterward receive me to glory.
> Whom have I in heaven but thee? And there is none upon earth that I desire besides thee.

My flesh and my heart faileth: but God is the strength of my heart, and my portion for ever.

PSALMS 73:22–26

Do not envy those who give in to temptation and have their physical appetites temporarily satisfied, and do not envy those who say they have never known temptation.

God's Word tells us that it is better to know temptation and overcome it, than to claim no knowledge of it:

> Blessed is the man that endureth temptation: for when he is tried, he shall receive the crown of life, which the Lord hath promised to them that love him.
>
> Let no man say when he is tempted, I am tempted of God: for God cannot be tempted with evil, neither tempteth he any man:
>
> But every man is tempted, when he is drawn away of his own lust, and enticed.
>
> Then when lust hath conceived, it bringeth forth sin: and sin, when it is finished, bringeth forth death.
>
> Do not err, my beloved brethren.

JAMES 1:12–16

There are some days when you feel spiritually weak; you know there are certain desires you should not give in to, but you don't think you are strong enough to withstand them.

Remember that the Scriptures tell us that God gives us only such burdens as He knows we can bear:

> There hath no temptation taken you but such as is common to man: but God is faithful, who will not suffer you to be tempted above that ye are able; but will with the temptation also make a way to escape, that ye may be able to bear it.

I CORINTHIANS 10:13

The next time you doubt your own ability to withstand temptation, remember that you do not stand alone. You are armored in righteousness, faith, and the promise of salvation brought to you by our Holy Redeemer:

> Stand therefore, having your loins girt about with truth, and having on the breastplate of righteousness;
> And your feet shod with the preparation of the gospel of peace;
> Above all, taking the shield of faith, wherewith ye shall be able to quench all the fiery darts of the wicked.
> And take the helmet of salvation, and the sword of the Spirit, which is the word of God.
>
> EPHESIANS 6:14–17

> Put on the whole armor of God, that ye may be able to stand against the wiles of the devil.
>
> EPHESIANS 6:11

There may be times when you are awake for many nights. You yearn with your body to give in to temptation, and you yearn with your soul to avoid it. The Scriptures tell us that we must curb physical urges and follow our spiritual needs instead:

> Let not sin therefore reign in your mortal body, that ye should obey it in the lusts thereof.
>
> ROMANS 6:12

The next time you are tempted, understand that the pleasure you seek will be yours just for the moment, but if you can deny that temptation, you will come to God, through Jesus Christ, and be happy with Him forever:

> Love not the world, neither the things that are in the world. If any man love the world, the love of the Father is not in him.
> For all that is in the world, the lust of the flesh, and the lust of the eyes, and the pride of life, is not of the Father, but is of the world.

And the world passeth away, and the lust thereof: but he that doeth the will of God abideth for ever.

I JOHN 2:15–17

Often, temptation appears garbed in beauty—indeed, if the beauty were not there, there would be no temptation! But what lies beneath that beauty? Is there a true spirit within, or does the outer shell hide an evil heart? Look beneath the surface of what is being offered to you—and consider the motivations, and the results of your actions should you succumb:

> Beware of false prophets, which come to you in sheep's clothing, but inwardly they are ravening wolves.
> Ye shall know them by their fruits. Do men gather grapes of thorns, or figs of thistles?
> Even so every good tree bringeth forth good fruit; but a corrupt tree bringeth forth evil fruit.
> A good tree cannot bring forth evil fruit, neither can a corrupt tree bring forth good fruit.
> Every tree that bringeth not forth good fruit is hewn down, and cast into the fire.
> Wherefore by their fruits ye shall know them.
>
> MATTHEW 7:15–20

Always try to act in accordance with God's wishes. You know that He wants you to do the right thing, and we are instructed:

> Submit yourself therefore to God. Resist the devil, and he will flee from you.
>
> JAMES 4:7

Perhaps you have overcome temptation of one particular sort more than a hundred times. Do not be proud of yourself, because you can be faced with other enticements that may be of more interest to you. Do not be smug about your virtues. The Bible advises us rather to be vigilant of other pitfalls that surround us:

> Be sober, be vigilant; because your adversary the devil, as a roaring lion, walked about, seeking whom he may devour.
>
> I PETER 5:8

All of us want gratification of one kind or another. It is because of this that temptations are so varied. However, if we can turn from physical gratification toward gratification of the spirit, we move that much closer to God and His Son.

Whatever tempts you, try to conquer it by reading and remembering:

> For they that are after the flesh do mind the things of the flesh; but they that are after the Spirit, the things of the Spirit.
> For to be carnally minded is death; but to be spiritually minded is life and peace.
>
> ROMANS 8:5–6

As children, we often use the phrase "I want," or "Give me now!" But as children, we don't know what is good for us, and our parents have to make sure that we are kept from harm.

As adults, it is up to us to exercise self-control. As the Word of God tells us:

> When I was a child, I spake as a child, I understood as a child, I thought as a child: but when I became a man, I put away childish things.
>
> I CORINTHIANS 13:11

Realize that now, as an adult, you have a responsibility to yourself and to our Saviour who loves you. We have

been told to put temptation from us and to look forward
to our life eternal with Him.

To help you in escaping the urges of the flesh and self-
indulgent needs, turn to God in faithfulness and with
trust:

> My soul, wait thou only upon God; for my expecta-
> tion is from him.
> He only is my rock and my salvation: he is my de-
> fense; I shall not be moved.
> In God is my salvation and my glory: the rock of my
> strength, and my refuge, is in God.
>
> PSALMS 62:5-7

The life of the Spirit, which we all so long for, can be
yours:

> For if ye live after the flesh, ye shall die: but if ye
> through the Spirit do mortify the deeds of the body, ye
> shall live.
>
> ROMANS 8:13

Remember His promise of life everlasting made over
and over again to you, and it shall be proof against temptation.

BIBLICAL SOURCES
AND REFERENCES

The Biblical passages throughout this book are taken from the King James Version (1611) of the Holy Bible. The King James Version was chosen because of the authors' familiarity with the text.

The Biblical passages that appear in this book have not been changed; however, in a very few cases, spelling has been modernized for the purpose of greater readability.

Following is an Index of all the Biblical passages used in *Bible Therapy*. The passages are listed as they appear in the Bible—by book, chapter, and verse.

An index of opening lines (see page 243) is also included for the convenience of those readers who wish to find a specific Biblical passage quickly.

Index of Biblical Passages

THE BOOKS OF THE OLD TESTAMENT

GENESIS

4:14–16, *144*	21:12–13, *112*	25:17, 22
5:3–5, 23	21:14–19, *113*	27:38–40 *84*
5:21–24, 23	23:1, *21*	39:21–23, *84*
19:31–33, 27	24:1, 22	
21:8–10, *112*	25:7–8, 22	

EXODUS

3:7–10, *151*	20:12, 25	23:9, *153*
8:1, 52	20:17, *78*	
13:21–22, 52	22:21, *165*	

LEVITICUS

19:17, *167*	19:18, *191*

NUMBERS

6:24–26, *43*

DEUTERONOMY

4:30–31, *176*	31:8, *51*	34:7, 20
8:7–10, *30*	31:23, *116*	34:10–12, 20
8:11–18, *31*	32:7, *19*	
24:19–22, *107*	33:27, *150*	

THE BOOKS OF THE NEW TESTAMENT

Index of Opening Lines

INDEX OF
PERSONAL PROBLEMS

As you have seen from the Contents, *Bible Therapy* is divided alphabetically into various sections, each one dealing with a specific problem that may beset you, and many people, today.

We think that you will find more than one section helpful when you are troubled. Here are some suggestions as to how you may use your *Bible Therapy*.

If you are bereaved by the passing of a loved one, turn to the section "Bereavement" and, for greater solace, continue your reading with the sections "Death and Dying," "Depression and Despair," "Sorrow and Anguish."

If you are depressed, read the section "Depression," and then follow with that section which pertains to the specific cause of your depression, such as "Poverty," "Crises," "Rejection," or any other section that seems applicable.

Bible Therapy is here to help you. Check the following Index of Personal Problems whenever you are troubled. It has been designed to make comforting and pertinent passages from the Bible available to you more quickly.